"Zachary Moon shows us how to build bridges where gulfs and gaps often exist between congregations and veterans and their families. Moon paves a way to bring the resources and strengths arising from military service into congregational life. He links the rich resources of congregations to veterans coming home. This well-written and usable book takes veterans and congregations into territory that they will be relieved to discover and inhabit together."

—Larry Graham, Iliff School of Theology

"This book will help congregations bring military service members and their families home—really home. For such homecomings both congregations and service members need to be transformed. This book will guide in that process toward healing and wholeness. We've been waiting for this book."

—Sharon Watkins, General Minister and President,
Disciples of Christ (Christian Church)

"*Coming Home* is THE book for people of faith who want to start a ministry to military personnel and their families. The theological reflections coupled with practical suggestions and resources make this book an ideal study guide for small groups or individuals. I wish this book had been available for the congregations I served as pastor!"

— Col. Robert C. Leivers, Chaplain,
U.S. Air Force Reserve (retired)

"Chaplain Moon writes: 'Recovery and restoration are a process like tending a house you live in.' As I continued to reintegrate, I had no idea the extent of the punishment that my own house had taken. A volume such as Zachary Moon's *Coming Home* would have been invaluable upon my return. I would have handed a copy to every member of my congregation. It is not that they were not loving, caring, accepting, and welcoming but more that we all just wanted to get back to 'normal' as quickly as possible. *Coming Home* would have shown us, and given us the permission, to take our time.

Chaplain Moon's *Coming Home* speaks frankly to the underlying issues of welcoming our veterans back into our communities. The text, the personal and small group discussion questions, and the veterans' reflections lead the reader through a well-defined and insightful process of coming to a personal, and communal, understanding of the feelings one may have about war and about those who engage in our wars. Chaplain Moon encourages the reader to welcome veterans and their families home into community without assumptions and preconceived notions of an individual experience. He encourages us to walk with the veteran and their family through the good and bad times. And he celebrates; the good news in all of this is that life, post-redeployment home, can be even more resolute through healthy reintegration."

—Stephen Boyd, Chaplain (Col.-retired),
U.S. Army Reserve, Minister for Chaplains and
Specialized Ministers, United Church of Christ

"Home, as a metaphor, describes that which is worth living for and dying for simultaneously. Using the metaphor of 'coming home,' which is as much a metaphor for the inward faith journey as it is a physical journey from one geography to another, Moon offers a great gift to the nation as he walks both congregants and veterans alike through a much-needed paradigm shift on how to develop ministries for our returning military men and women. Presenting a comprehensive picture of the psycho-social-spiritual dynamics and witness of military personnel and their families, he carefully sensitizes the reader to the cultural nuances of military life as he introduces helpful perspectives on how returning veterans and congregants can, through mutuality, both find the way home as people of faith."
—Lee Butler, Chicago Theological Seminary

"Within the peace-church tradition, so many of us are completely ill-equipped to respond lovingly or helpfully to members of the military or their families. Because of our inability to see beyond the war and violence we reject, we miss the opportunity to see individuals who may actually share our passionate quest for peace, purpose, community—and God. Zachary Moon's *Coming Home* refocuses our attention on the person now home from battle and wondering if there is a place for them in our congregation. The combination of story, biblical references, and reflection questions makes this a very useful resource for faith communities interested in learning to accompany military personnel along a healing and transformation journey we all need."
—Colin Saxton, General Secretary, Friends United Meeting

"News reports often focus on the needs and problems of military service members, veterans, and their families, compelling people of faith to reach out and help. Chaplain Zachary Moon says that such help will likely be rejected if congregations only see service members as wounded. He challenges congregations to set aside a 'helper-victim' approach to pastoral care fostered by the media. His readily accessible text invites congregations into a relational process of pastoral care that begins with their own experiences and beliefs about military service and war. Readers are invited to bring their beliefs into dialogue with a range of Christian perspectives on military service and war. He collaborates with service members and veterans in providing a series of biblical conversations about what it means to make space in our hearts and pews for service members and their families. This relational process of care creates church homes that can truly welcome and honor the unique stories and strengths of service members, veterans, and their families. *Coming Home* is a unique and highly needed resource for congregations whose faith moves them to reach out in love and caring to military service members, veterans, and their families."

—Carrie Doehring, Iliff School of Theology

"*Coming Home* is an excellent resource for individuals, study groups, mission committees, and congregational care teams in faith communities who want to engage in informed and caring relationships with military service persons, veterans, and their families. Chaplain Moon offers a compelling and richly thoughtful invitation into such ministries. He helps readers recognize that walking beside those coming home from war and their families gives congregations opportunities to deepen faith and practice."

—Nancy J. Ramsay, Brite Divinity School

COMING HOME

Ministry That Matters with Veterans and Military Families

Zachary Moon

CHALICE
PRESS

ST. LOUIS, MISSOURI

Bible quotations marked NRSV are from the *New Revised Standard Version Bible,* copyright 1989, Division of Christian Education of the National Council of the Churches of Christ in the United States of America. Used by permission. All rights reserved.

Scripture quotations marked (NIV) are taken from the HOLY BIBLE, NEW INTERNATIONAL VERSION®. NIV®. Copyright © 1973, 1978, 1984 by International Bible Society. Used by permission of Zondervan Publishing House. All rights reserved.

Bible quotations marked KJV are from the *King James Version Bible.*

Cover art and design: Rohaan Malhotra

www.ChalicePress.com

Print: 9780827205383   EPUB: 9780827205390   EPDF: 9780827205406

Library of Congress Cataloging-in-Publication Data

Moon, Zachary.
  Coming home : ministry that matters with veterans and military families / Zachary Moon. —1st [edition].
    pages cm
  ISBN 978-0-8272-0538-3 (pbk.)
1. Church work with military personnel. 2. Church work with veterans. 3. Church work with families. I. Title.

BV4457.M66 2015
259.088'355—dc23

2014045092

Contents

Acknowledgments

My deepest gratitude to all those who shared their voices, insight, and wisdom in the writing and rewriting of this project.

To my many faithful brothers and sisters in the Chaplain Corps, the sailors and Marines and their families, in whose company I am blessed to serve.

To the communities that raised me—the Religious Society of Friends, Faith Community Church, Camas Friends Church, and the Christian Church (Disciples of Christ).

To my parents and the many loving people who are my family.

To my wife, son, and daughter.

My life is possible only because of you.

Thank you.

Foreword

Congregations using this guide will discover how to be better friends to all those we love, and we will become stronger communities in the process. We will more deeply incarnate a life-giving, transformative wholeness in a larger society anxious about the future, reactive to threats, resigned to disposable relationships, and distracted by consumerism. This is holy work indeed.

I first met Zachary Moon at the Riverside Church in New York on March 20, 2010, where we were serving as Commissioners for the Truth Commission on Conscience in War. He was finishing his M.Div. degree and working as a Veterans Affairs chaplain. As our Commission deliberations proceeded, I was struck by his seriousness of purpose, his perceptive listening abilities, and his deep concern and respect for military veterans and families, commitments that are evident in this book.

Since then, Zachary has deepened his understanding of how to support those who serve in the military and its veterans, as well as their families and communities. He offers us the wisdom he has gained through his previous work as a VA chaplain and his current vocation as a Navy chaplain. In addition, he brings insights from his intellectual work as a scholar of pastoral theology and care.

Readers will find in these pages a valuable guide to being a better friend to those who, like my own father, serve their country and come home from war forever changed. If this book had existed in 1968, my relationship with my father, our entire family, and my adult life would have been very different—and, I know with certainty, transformed for the better. I am glad this book has finally been written. We all need it.

Rita Nakashima Brock

Are We Ready for
Our Veterans?

The unique and needed role of congregations in the reintegration process for veterans and military families was made clear to me early in my work as a chaplain. I was working at a VA hospital, and a young combat vet asked to talk. He was at the VA that day to see his primary care doctor, who recommended he see the psychiatrist for a screening for post-traumatic stress disorder. He began our conversation by saying, "Chaplain, they're gonna tell me I'm crazy. I'm not crazy. I'm just dealing with some things." I worked with many vets with PTSD diagnoses, and I could see that he was exhibiting many of the symptoms that substantiate that diagnosis, but I could also hear that he wanted to be seen as more than those symptoms, more than his suffering. He entrusted me with his story, and it changed the way I understood my work.

He grew up with a church being the center of his life, a guiding and loving community that helped him grow into adulthood. He enlisted after graduating from high school and spent much of his deployment in Iraq serving as military police. Since returning from deployment, he was struggling to integrate his experiences in combat with the day-to-day life he found back at home. And his wife and kids were trying to figure it out, too—how to bring this member of their family back into a meaningful role and connected part in their lives after his absence.

Because he had mentioned the importance of his church and his faith, as the conversation continued, I asked him what role his spirituality and church had in his life since his return from Iraq. He said his home church was the first place he went, bringing with him excitement and expectation. He had been separated not only from his family but also from this loving group of folks, and he looked forward to being reunited. But as he sat in his spot in the pew and looked around at these folks who had known him his whole life and helped him become the man he was today, he did not experience relief.

His combat experiences had changed him, not just in harmful ways, but in many significant and strengthening ways. In combat, he had been with a community of brothers and sisters who stood shoulder to shoulder in the worst circumstances, who lived out the meaning of Jesus' teaching that "there is no greater love than to lay down one's life for a friend." He wanted church to be willing to practice what they preached, and what he witnessed when he returned to church was a bunch of nice folks sitting passively in the pews without much regard for those around them. He said that everyone was living in their own bubble. He said he felt betrayed.

That day I felt I could help him by hearing his story and responding with my perspective on what God thinks about our wellbeing. I told him that I believed that God wants us to be healthy and whole, wants us to have the support we need, and wouldn't want anything to get in the way of that. We talked about the stigma around mental health and how it is sometimes hard to navigate the VA system to get what you need.

But his story lingered in my mind. What kind of church was he looking for? What would a church need to become that sort of community? He and I had grown up in very different Christian traditions, but I understood his experience of feeling unseen and of needing more from his church family but being unable to ask.

I have been on both sides of this encounter. I grew up in a liberal Christian community that was deeply committed to pacifism and viewed military service quite negatively. As I grew up I came to believe that this approach was problematic, particularly in terms of engaging the human experience of war and the real cost of military service. During my seminary education, I began chaplaining at a VA hospital. And then, following graduation, I took a chaplain job at another VA hospital. A little more than a year later, I was commissioned as a military chaplain. There were times when my religious upbringing felt at odds with ministry in a military environment. But what surprised me most was how little any of that mattered, as long as I was aware of it, stayed in the conversation, and was willing to meet individuals where they were, for who they were.

As I did this work, I realized that as a chaplain I had only a brief time to accompany each person on his or her journey. Where would they land next? Would they find the support they needed? I recognized that many churches didn't know where to begin in reaching out and receiving returning combat veterans, not because they didn't want to, but because they didn't see how to do it effectively.

Churches have a unique and powerful contribution to make: engaging in our rich traditions and practices, engaging with one another, and making meaning and integrating the many experiences life throws at us. Together, the Body of Christ is stronger than any of its individual members.

Military service members and their families need our attention. They need space in the pews of our churches and room in our hearts. Whatever they are dealing with, they are people just like us. We need to bring them home—not just back from overseas, but home.

This will be a transformative process of reorienting, not just for the service member and his/her family, but for all of us. We need to say more than, "Thank you for your service." We need to find ways of saying, with our words and our actions, "We are excited that you are here. We have been waiting for you. We have a meaningful role for you to play in our community. Together, in this relationship, we can create something that wasn't possible before. Thanks be to God!"

Seemingly, every day there are new headlines about growing rates of suicide, domestic violence, unemployment, homelessness, and slowness in gaining medical services for veterans. As our nation seeks to address these matters, new threats abroad remind us that the demands of military service are never far away.

Many good folks are gaining awareness of some of the issues and are concerned, but how can we best engage and contribute? There are as many ways to contribute as there are people who have the heart to do so. Remember the call to prophetic work received by Jeremiah—we need to remove barriers and build new possibilities (Jeremiah 1:10).

Military service involves complex human experiences that don't easily fit into boxes or categories. Some reflecting and reorienting are necessary for us to do this community work effectively. If all of our knowledge is acquired from the media coverage and other sources that focus primarily on post-traumatic stress, traumatic brain injury, instances of suicide, and so on, we may come to see our service members as victims of their combat experiences who need our help to heal.

This "helper-victim" approach is problematic and will likely repel and exclude most military service members because most of them don't think of themselves as injured or ill. Although most church communities are well versed in how to do charity work, that is not what is needed from us at this time; the opportunity here is to become more deeply receptive and responsive in relationship, to reach out and meet folks where they are, and to embrace their full personhood and experiences.

This book explores issues related to military service and how congregations can best reintegrate and engage military service members and their families. These are not simple matters, and there are no simple answers. It is not the intention of this book to prescribe the agenda or dictate the action plan for you, because the most vital responses will come from each congregation, discerning its gifts and building meaningful relationships.

To fully realize this opportunity, we need to do some reflective work both as individuals and as communities of faith. We have rich gifts, which we may have not yet recognized, to offer to military families. And we may have some barriers, which we haven't considered, to building relationships with those serving in the military. This reflection and preparation is part of the needed reorienting process. Instead of just learning about combat experiences and veterans' hardships, we need to begin with ourselves: our experiences, our beliefs, and our spiritual gifts.

Once we have completed this inventory as individuals and as communities, we can better grasp where we stand, who we are, and what we can do. Just as important, we can better hear the experiences of others and engage in conversation. Or, to say it differently, the work of relationship isn't about gathering lots of bits of information about the person you want to meet; it begins by looking within ourselves and then meeting that person for who he or she is. When we better understand who we are, we will be better listeners and better communicators. And that's what we need to build relationships.

This book is designed for small groups to easily engage it for study and conversation. Each of the following six chapters provides exploration of an important area and is accompanied by discussion questions that will support further reflection and dialogue. The appendix includes five biblical reflections and recommendations for further reading.

Here are just some of the ways to utilize this book:

- Personal study;
- Small group study, such as adult religious education;
- Background for a sermon series;
- Reflection and theological education within a seminary context.

Whether you are a military service member, veteran, member of a military family, a chaplain working in this field of ministry, a pastor, or a civilian concerned for the wellbeing of military service members and their families, this book has something to offer you.

- Chapter 1 introduces traditional Christian beliefs about war and invites you to take an inventory of personal experiences that inform your thinking about war and those in the military.
- Chapter 2 unpacks important elements of military culture, including motivation for enlistment, the process of training and identity formation, and the specific language, symbols, and practices that make life in the military culturally distinct from civilian life.
- Chapter 3 examines the human experiences of combat and the many ways participating in war can impact people.
- Chapter 4 considers the unique experiences of military families, including the opportunities of military life and the challenges of the deployment cycle.
- Chapter 5 concerns our pastoral responses to veterans and military families, focusing on a strengths-based approach.

- Chapter 6 explores options for taking action, and how individually and as a church community we can engage in receptive and responsive ministry.

One of the goals of this project is to dynamically connect your personal experience, the resources of your faith tradition, and the active role you can enact in responsive ministry with veterans and military families. You will find many questions in this book and very few prescriptive solutions to the challenges that lay ahead. This is intentional. There aren't any quick fix-its, and to forward a single agenda or program for all congregations would be as foolish as asserting that all veterans and military family members need the same thing.

The hope that I carry and that sustains a book like this is that you will take the time to thoughtfully reflect and discern how God is leading your response and that we will develop a diversity of ministries that are deeply rooted in our particular communities. I believe the gifts and resources each congregation needs to get involved are already present. Our task is to join together and faithfully knock at the doors God has placed before us.

As those doors open, congregations will find many ways they can accompany military families throughout their lives, providing a space that encourages reflection, learning, and integration. Congregations, the living witnesses to God's grace-filled presence in human experience, can embrace the whole person, because God's love has no bounds. Our nation's veterans and their families may already be in your congregations, while many others would seek to join your community. Whatever your background, opportunities for meaningful relationship are available if you answer the call.

1

★ ★ ★

War and Those Who Fight

Be willing to put beliefs and theories and doctrine on the shelf and
see the person standing before you. Pastors are first responders, they
hold the power of life and death in their hands and all too often fail
to realize it. Words can create or destroy, so use them sparingly. Show
the military community that you love them by acting lovingly. Create
spaces in which congregations can hear the stories. The wisdom our
veterans carry home from war is not their own to carry, it belongs to the
church. **Logan Martin Isaac**

Our experiences and our beliefs shape what we think about war.
In any church community there will be many different backgrounds
and perspectives. Differences can be a great opportunity to learn, and
it is important for us to have a personal awareness of the experiences
each one of us brings. Part of the process in preparing to be more open
and less stuck in unhelpful judgments and expectations is to become
more aware of our own deeply held views. Doing a personal inventory
is a necessary first step in clarifying what in your background informs
your thinking about war and those who serve in the military. Take
some time to reflect on these questions:

1. What are my personal experiences with the military?
2. What are my family's experiences with the military?
3. What are my thoughts, values, and beliefs about war?
4. What are my thoughts and beliefs about those who serve and have served in the military?

Our particular backgrounds, values, and beliefs shape our personal perspectives, but they also impact how we react and respond to another person's story.

Further reflection may be important as well. For example, have you consciously thought about these questions before? Did you find your answers to these questions came out quickly or slowly?

Clarifying and connecting with our own experiences makes us more available and receptive in connecting with another's experiences. If our hope and intention is to authentically engage with veterans and their families, we need to be thoughtful about how our unexamined attitudes may be resources or barriers to relationship.

This reflective work may illuminate previously hidden elements that shape our thinking. Delving into our backgrounds, reflecting on deeply held beliefs and values, and challenging assumptions about others can bring out all kinds of feelings, some of which are uncomfortable. As important as it is not to let judgment of others keep us from engaging in relationship with them, it is just as important not to let judgment of ourselves keep us from getting started. You need to be compassionate and forgiving toward yourself. You also need to be intentional about the religious and spiritual practices that help to sustain you when you are doing challenging reflective work.

Reading this book and hearing some of the stories and experiences within it may generate conflicting thoughts and emotions. Your impulse may be to look for quick answers or to push past what is coming up to you. In these moments, try instead to slow down and pay attention. Listen. Something deeper may be right below the surface that will help you in this reorienting process. Take some time now to reflect on these two questions:

1. What religious or spiritual practices help me when I experience barriers with others?

2. What religious or spiritual practices help me when I encounter another's stress or suffering?

Spiritual practices can connect and ground us in God's love and grace. Particularly when we encounter a person who has different experiences, values, or beliefs, we may feel uncomfortable and even anxious. This is a prime moment to return to the spiritual practices that bring us back to calm so that we can be open to hearing and be compassionately responsive.

Hearing another person's story is sacred work. It involves trust. That person is taking a risk to tell you his or her story, and you are taking a risk to stay open and listen. Without question, military service changes those who serve and those who love them. However, no two veterans have had identical experiences. Making assumptions about someone's experience is a misstep and may betray the trust that has been extended to us.

What a veteran will want to share of his/her experiences will vary greatly. Like any of us, there are stories that we share with others easily, while there are other stories we may never share, even with our most trusted loved ones. Granting this, it is still the case that trust is usually the most significant factor in what and how we share. Moreover, we honor another's trust when we listen with compassion and are slow to judgment. The great poet Rumi stated: "Out beyond ideas of wrongdoing and rightdoing there is a field. I'll meet you there." This is a spirit needed to nurture authentic relationships.

Christian Perspectives on War

Listening is not a neutral activity. We interpret what we hear and we make judgments about it. Our interpretations and our judgments are at least partly shaped by our preexisting beliefs.

Christian traditions have had divergent theological perspectives on the subject of war. Some of these perspectives may inform our own attitudes toward war and those who participate in war.

Below you will find some background on three views of war. This is a very brief survey of Christian perspectives, but it does provide some useful discussion of the traditional theological streams that still fuel our Christian identity.

Pacifism

In the early church, a refusal to fight or participate in any way in war-making was a part of a larger resistance to, and withdrawal from, worldly life and the institutions of the Roman Empire. Early Christians were discouraged—at times even forbidden—from military service. With devotion to a "Prince of Peace," how could one be violent? But pacifismBut Christian resistance to violence was not an absolutist position, even during these early generations. Some soldiers continued in their military service after conversion and were accepted by the church and served communion.

Pacifism is a much more recent term, and it does not necessarily include a religious basis for resistance to violence and war, although many of the great leaders in nonviolence have looked to Christian history and the teachings and actions of Jesus for inspiration. Christian pacifists see Jesus teaching his followers to "not resist the evildoer. But if anyone strikes you on the right cheek, turn the other also" (Mt. 5:39). They hear Jesus preaching, "Love your enemies and pray for those who persecute you" (v. 44). Pacifism is not simply the valuing of peace above war or other forms of violence; it is the total refusal of using violent means of response.

The Christian pacifist vision has been renewed in the centuries since Jesus and the witness of the early church. Saint Francis of Assisi, the Anabaptist Movement during the later stages of the Protestant Reformation, Thomas Merton, Martin Luther King Jr., and Archbishop Oscar Romero are all key contributors in the traditions of Christian pacifism.

Many others have employed nonviolence as a strategy for social change, not because of its religious virtue but because nonviolent means were the most pragmatic tactic to bring about the intended results. This approach may overlap with a religious principle of pacifism, but it may also stand alone. Christian pacifism would claim that refusing violent action is required regardless of conditions, circumstances, or results. The Christian pacifist would point to Jesus' command to love our enemies and would draw the conclusion that there is never a time, situation, or goal that would justify violence.

Holy War

After Emperor Constantine's conversion in 312 C.E., the role of Christianity shifted significantly in the social and political context of that time. Violence played a crucial role in the expansion and control of the vast Roman Empire, and new theological ideas and justifications began to emerge that could justify the use of force.

Christian Holy War became fully manifest hundreds of years later with the waging of the Crusades. More than ever before, war took on a religious rationale for Christians. They weren't only fighting for their country but for their God. The enemy was not only a threat to their material wellbeing but to their eternal souls. Christianity was used as the primary resource to recruit for, motivate, and mobilize war-fighting

There are also adaptations of the Holy War vision in more recent times. Looking at the history of the United States through a religious lens, there is evidence that many early American settlers were drawing on the idea of God-endorsed coercion and conquest when they forced indigenous peoples from their homeland. These settlers saw themselves as God-chosen people destined to control and occupy God-chosen land no matter the loss of life to peoples seen as heathens.

There is biblical material that appears to substantiate such Holy War action. Consider God's statement to the Israelites when the land of Canaan was given to them by divine authority, even though it was populated by other people. The invading Israelites were to "utterly destroy them. Make no covenant with them and show them no mercy" (Deut. 7:2). In the book of Judges, the prophetess Deborah testified to God's desire for war against Sisera's army, and in the aftermath of battle, Deborah's song glorifies the victory and concludes, "so perish all your enemies, O Lord!" (Judg. 5:31).

The justification of Holy War is powerful in its simplicity. War does not belong to us, but belongs to God and the forces of good must defeat forces of evil. Further, the enemy ceases to maintain any human characteristic and is instead the adversary of God. Therefore, there are no restraints or moral ambiguities in war-making.

Particularly in our time in history, such theology of war lends itself toward engaging in total war, waged not only against combatants but the entire society and culture deemed enemy.

Just War

Just War is perhaps the best known Christian position on war and falls between the previous two perspectives. The Just War doctrine details certain requirements for going to war and how to wage it. To go to war: (1) it must be a clear response to intentional and injurious aggression by another; (2) the overall damage of the war must not exceed the original injury suffered; (3) it must be waged by the legitimate government of a nation; (4) it must have righteous intention, with restoring peace as the overarching moral obligation; (5) it must be as a last resort following the attempt and failure of diplomatic measures; and, (6) it must have the probability of succeeding in all these areas. In the waging of war, proportionality is always the mandate: the means must be proportional to the ends, meaning the weapons used must be proportional to their target and not cause unnecessary damage and loss of life. Proportionality recognizes the intrinsic value of life, even when that life is deemed your enemy.

One would be hard-pressed to argue that any war ever met these criteria in full. The modernizing of warfare and development of weapon technology, such as bombs, missiles, machine guns, drones, and many others, has drastically changed how wars are fought and would make it very difficult to meet Just War requirements. Yet this doctrine has continued to be used by political leaders and military strategists—as well as religious communities—when engaging the moral challenges of entering into and waging war.

There are some very important underlying assumptions to this approach. Firstly, there is an acknowledgment that war-making can get out of hand, and therefore there ought to be some principles to govern military action. Such limits, like not killing noncombatants, may aid a sustainable peace in the years following war, a worthy goal that sometimes gets lost in the fog of modern warfare. Parameters of military engagement can also provide a framework for international negotiations between nations. But even this possibility has been greatly tested by the conditions of "The War on Terror," where the enemy is not a nation, but a system of roaming insurgent organizations.

The justification of war-making has not been a simple project for Christians, then or now. Perhaps none of these perspectives are adequate to the task, but you can see how concern for the moral questions raised by war-making has been sought to be reconciled with religious values. Just as different Christian traditions have read the Bible with different interpretations or have understood sacramental practices differently, different Christian perspectives have emerged in the face of the moral demands created by war-making.

Now we face these moral demands and must reflect for ourselves and as church communities how we should understand these issues and respond. Values and beliefs drive our personal choices and actions, and shape how we see the choices and actions of others. Christianity lacks a single, unified position on war and those who fight, but the histories and theologies of various Christian traditions provide much that impacts our thinking today. It is important to understand our history as we reflect on our own positions and perspectives on such significant issues.

Discussion Questions

Personal inventory questions:

1. What are my personal experiences with the military? What are my family's experiences with the military?
2. What are my thoughts, values, and beliefs about war?
3. What are my thoughts and beliefs about those who serve and have served in the military?
4. What religious or spiritual practices sustain me when I experience barriers with others?

Questions about Christian perspectives on war:

1. Where would you locate yourself in the spectrum of pacifism <–> just war <–> holy war?
2. Where are these perspectives supported in the Bible or in your church tradition?
3. What are some of the questions that these perspectives raise for you in your reflections about war and those who fight?

For small group discussion:

Consider sharing your reflections on the questions above. Also, it may be important to reflect on these matters:

1. What are our congregation's values and beliefs about war?
2. Where would we locate our congregation in the spectrum of pacifism <–> just war <–> holy war?
3. What are our congregation's values and beliefs about those who serve and have served in the military?

2

★ ★ ★

Bridging the Gap of Understanding

The military—like most denominations and churches—is deeply rooted in tradition. The military has its own customs and rituals, uses its own language and images, and operates within a given set of codes and values. Those who serve in the military are trained to integrate these customs, terminology, and values into their identity. Military service is more than a job; it is an entire way of life.

Why Do People Join the Military?

I was a senior in college and saw all my buddies going into banking or insurance or the stock market or law, and I wanted to do something exciting that would make a difference to my country, so I chose Navy Intelligence. My grandfather was in the Navy in WWII, my dad was a Marine just prior to Vietnam, and so the Navy seemed best for me.
Charlie Conway

I joined the military for more than one reason. I came from a military family—both my father and my mother were military. I am bred, born, and raised military. I remember very distinctly being 5 years old or so and being asked what I wanted to do when I grew up. Every time, my answer was "soldier." Then when I was seventeen, I enlisted because it was the quickest, surest, and most legitimate way to run away from home. *Sarah Schott*

Different generations of veterans have joined the military for different reasons. Even during wars when the draft was in effect, many of those who fought volunteered. After the events of September 11, 2001, there was a wave of military enrollment, much like there was after the bombing of Pearl Harbor. There was a sense among many that our country had been attacked, and there was a clear need to respond militarily in defense of national security. Patriotism is a part of why many men and women join the military, but there are also other reasons. For many young people the military appears to be the best, and sometimes only, opportunity for meaningful work, financial well-being, and college education.

I grew up on an east Texas farm. Our home was literally not more than a stone's throw away from a pigpen. In middle school, I often dreamed of going to college and seeing the world. By the time I was 12 years old, I was calling various colleges and universities requesting information. Some told me I was way too young. But a couple of them responded and sent me their catalogues. Receiving correspondence in the mail from a university was like Christmas to me.

During my senior year I was devastated when my father called me out onto the porch. With hogs squealing in the background and the pungent odor in the air, he informed me that there was no money for school. My heart sank. I tossed and turned the entire night. The next morning I called a Navy recruiter. *Jamie Hawley*

Recruiting efforts promote messages such as, "It takes a multi-tiered force of highly trained, committed Soldiers to protect our freedoms and uphold democracy" (www.goarmy.com/about/service-options.html); or, "We turn the willing into the able, transforming purpose-driven recruits into Marines who make a difference. Only those who complete the most demanding training can accomplish the world's most demanding missions. If you seek our title, the path ahead will be one of great challenge. Prevail, and your proudest days will be realized" (www.marines.com/becoming-a-marine). These messages focus on ideals and values such as freedom, democracy, commitment, accomplishment, and pride. The opportunity provided is not just a job, but a unique and transformative experience.

> Growing up I always wanted to be in the medical field and in the military. My Grandpa was in the Army in WWII in Hawaii and I wanted to be just like him. In my senior year of high school my mom told me she would not co-sign for student loans, and that same week the Navy recruiter called me and said he wanted to give me a $30k scholarship. **Michelle Hart**

> In 1967, I landed in front of a Circuit Court Judge. Since I was an adult in my home state at 17, I was given an option of 4 years in jail or 4 years in military service. The Judge didn't care which option I took as long as I got out of town and stayed out for at least 4 years. I decided that military service sounded just fine to me. **Al Hendrix**

Remember being seventeen or eighteen? What was your life about? Homework assignments, household chores, who was taking whom to the school dance, what the heck you would do after high school. Take a moment and let your mind reorient to what you were thinking about, worrying about, and wishing for. Recruitment materials are designed to engage that mindset: "Obstacles once considered insurmountable are now passable. The determination to prevail now overpowers the desire to quit. As you begin to change, you will not lose your soul—you will discover it. Your identity will not be erased; it will be sharpened" (www.marines.com/becoming-a-marine). For many of us in our late teens, whether or not we ever considered military service at that juncture of our lives, this promise of purpose and power would have held great appeal.

No one single universal reason motivates all service members to join, and the background of each service member is unique. When speaking to a service member, one should not assume to know why he or she made the choice to enlist. It is also important to recognize that one's willingness to put on the uniform, be deployed abroad, and fire a weapon is not synonymous with a desire to kill. If you are looking for a place to begin understanding how to connect with those in the military, think about the willingness to serve. Think about what motivates someone to do any kind of community service, and make the sacrifices of time and personal comfort, and the many other adjustments that are required. Think about the sense of accomplishment and contribution you feel when you do something for someone else, not because you have to, but because you are willing to.

Probably all of us have had the experience of making a big life choice for a set of reasons and discovering other reasons along the way that we hadn't expected. Often our initial reason for becoming involved in something is not necessarily what keeps us there. But the whole story is important. Most persons who join the military are young adults; therefore, the experiences that they have during military service have a significant impact on who they become. Let's be willing to hear the whole story of someone's life rather than taking a hasty snapshot of who we think he or she is now.

Military Branches and Cultural Difference

Much of this book speaks of veterans in general and military families as a group. This is necessary in simplifying our exploration, but it is not adequate in other ways. The different branches of the military and the subsets within those branches are not a simple, unified body. They have different jobs and responsibilities, different histories and traditions, different languages and structures. Too many books, for example, use the term "soldier" to speak of those who serve in the military. This would bother many sailors, Marines, airmen, and coastguardsmen, because the term "soldier" is used only by the Army and is not a general term.

Language matters and can't be underestimated. Some terms are similar across military training, but for reasons dictated by the culture, customs, and needs of the branch and job within it, there are many distinct aspects. Each veteran we meet has his/her own story to tell, and we need to resist assuming that one veteran's experience is like another's.

Between veterans this difference in culture may show itself in competitive-sounding banter or salty humor. A kind of cultural hierarchy exists between branches of service that basically correlates to how close you were to the worst of it in combat. When a Marine describes the Air Force as "a great alternative to the military," it is more than just a joke; it is an acknowledgment of history and role. Marines have always and continue to identify themselves as the "First to Fight," and the ones who endure the corresponding loss of life and limb for being the "boots on the ground." This reality has informed the cultural identity that is integrated through boot camp and deepened through combat experience. The airman on the receiving end of this comment does not deserve to think less of his or her service, but such are the long-held norms between branches. While this explanation does not excuse such an interaction, it is meant to illustrate that calling one service member by the name of another branch of service may unintentionally frustrate or come off as ignorant.

Training and Identity Formation

Military training challenged me both physically and mentally in a way that schooling had not. In Basic Training, the harsh environment and close knit relationships it requires forced me to wrestle with what I was made of and whether I could accomplish unlikely physical goals. My best one-mile run time got down to 5 minutes and 15 seconds. Military training focused my mind and my body in ways and to degrees I had never before experienced, and I was incredibly proud of myself that I had shown I was capable of meeting the demands the military required. **Logan Martin Isaac**

Although different branches of the military and different jobs within the military have different training, most often called "basic training" or "boot camp," military training is a rite of passage for all who serve in uniform. Movies have depicted this training as a physically grueling event dictated by an overbearing disciplinarian drill instructor who constantly yells demeaning insults at the recruits. This is only part of the experience, and probably not the part that is most important to understand.

The long hikes, demanding challenges, and shouting have a purpose behind them. To prepare a person to take on the stressors of combat and other high-stakes kinds of work, a person needs to be stretched beyond what is comfortable. Recruits need to experience high levels of stress, so that when they experience stress down the road, they know how to manage it. Recruits need to experience fear, frustration, uncertainty, and exhaustion for the same reason. There are stories about this training being done incorrectly by leaders who don't understand how to test recruits without breaking them beyond repair. These tragic exceptions are not the rule of law. This high-stakes, high-stress training should be done with safety and discipline as its highest priorities—and this is generally what occurs.

> When I joined the Marines, the U.S. had been in a state of peace for quite a while. At the time there were no looming conflicts, but that quickly changed two months and eighteen days after I stood on the yellow footprints. In boot camp, our week on the range was scheduled for September 9–15; midway into the week I quickly grew up. What was formerly a three-month stint of training for the purpose of becoming "tough" turned into preparation for combat, something that became very real. My military training began to callous me to the world around. I lost sensitivity to hurt and pain in the world and began to live under the illusion that an effective warrior was a heartless warrior.
> **Patrick Stefan**

For those whose jobs in the military will involve the use of weapons and the possible taking of life, training is designed to give a person that capacity. Killing is something that must be learned in order to accomplish the mission deemed necessary in defense of our country. Those who are properly trained understand killing not to be morally insignificant, but rather necessary in certain circumstances. For most of us growing up, the use of violence was restricted only to instances of immediate defense of self and others. In combat, the principle of defense remains central and continues to view violence as a last resort, but applies the principle of defense to a larger scale of national security.

> My combat training changed me. It showed me how precious life is and how tenuous it is in a combat zone. I learned to pay attention to minute

details because if you don't (tie your bootlaces correctly, for example), it can cost you or a buddy dearly. **Charlie Conway**

Learning to kill and to manage stress, fear, and other emotions likely to emerge during military service are two of the key elements of military training. The third, and perhaps most transformative, is the building of unit cohesion. Americans are known for fierce individualism. Most of us have been habituated to think first of ourselves—our wants, needs, and desires—and seek personal accomplishment and acclaim. A military, however, cannot function as a group of individuals exercising personal wants and desires. The group must function as one unit at the highest levels of discipline and efficiency. If a member is caught up in his or her own agenda, the whole unit is at risk. Learning to follow orders and put the needs of the group and mission before one's personal needs is a sacrifice made by all members of the military. Military function is founded on good order and discipline. Good unit cohesion and function sounds like Paul's description of the Body of Christ in the first letter to the Corinthians: each member with a distinct role to play in animating its portion of the larger community.

My greatest learning happened specifically because of relationships I established with shipmates who did not hold my worldview, or have my identical life map, culture, background, beliefs, or values. Looking back, it was my shipmates, all of them, who helped me to "see" God from a much broader and bigger perspective. **Jamie Hawley**

This new kind of personhood is oriented to the community's success, and to accomplishing the mission at hand. And such persons could provide a special challenge when it comes to the life of our churches. If those in the pews who have not experienced the depth of trust and interdependency necessary to survive combat are open to it, there is the potential for great learning about the importance and potential of cohesion in our church communities. Perhaps most of us, if not all of us, have at times wished for greater support and more trusting relationships in our church home, especially at times of stressful life changes and transitions. Our churches don't need to be ready to convoy in a combat zone, but imagine if our church members learned to see the power of teamwork and having each other's back when times got tough. When congregations are at their best, the trials of life are not minimized or ignored, but become the rallying point for coming together and getting through by lifting up each other.

Many veterans struggle to find that kind of community when they get home from deployment. The sense of togetherness they knew in combat that contributed to their survival in the most dangerous environments is nowhere to be found. The rules and discipline that service members have integrated into their identity don't seem to apply, and there is a sense that only those who have "trained like I've trained, fought like I've fought, and been through what I've been through" are qualified to be trusted. This narrows the interpersonal world of veterans significantly, may keep them away from church and other supportive communities altogether, and lead to the kind of isolation that too often proves deadly.

How could our churches be more trustworthy and capable teams? Where do we need to train and develop ourselves so that our church team has the necessary cohesion to function at a high level? Are we willing to be challenged to make the kind of sacrifices that make this kind of trust and cohesion possible? Our answers to these questions may well reveal how open our church is to authentic relationship with veterans and their families.

Churches need to move beyond just thinking *they* have something to offer these veterans and their families. In reality, military service members have much to offer to their churches. The potential exists for a deeply mutual and beneficial relationship. The experiences of being in the military may have come with challenges of many kinds, but those who understand the ethos of military service, the focus and discipline, and the value of community cooperation have something to offer the life and mission of their congregation. Working together in relationship, with each member of the Body of Christ bringing his or her vital gift, we become stronger than we were before.

Discussion Questions

Personal Reflection:

1. What are my beliefs on why persons join the military?
2. What value judgments do I make about those who join?
3. What surprised me about this account of military culture and training?

For Small Group Discussion:

Consider sharing your reflections on the questions above. Also, it may be important to reflect on:

1. How could our congregation work to bridge gaps in our understanding about the experiences of veterans and military families?
2. How could our congregation deepen its teamwork and experience greater community cohesion?

3

★ ★ ★

Human Experiences
of Combat

When I came home, I attempted to transition right back into "regular life." In fact, most people didn't even acknowledge I was gone, with the exception of a few questions like, "How was it?" to which I answered, "What do you think?" Coming home was a massive challenge. I didn't sleep well for a long time, and I dealt with extreme bouts of anger, which I internalized. *Patrick Stefan*

In order to genuinely welcome service members home, we need to think in new ways about combat and the experiences of those who serve in the military. If you are a veteran, some of this may be very familiar. If your knowledge about war has been primarily shaped by the media, TV shows, and movies, some of this may help you see a bigger and more complex picture of what happens in combat.

No two veterans have the same experience, even those who wear the same uniform and fight in the same battle. It is true that the shared experience of combat may bond veterans to one another; however, this bond is not because they have had an identical experience, but because they have endured that danger and made the sacrifice of putting their lives at risk.

Service to Nation, Loyalty to Comrades

What could possibly compel someone to stay in harm's way and remain in the fight when suffering, injury, and even death seems overwhelmingly certain? Military training provides some simulation of this level of stress and builds the capacity for endurance, but one can never be totally prepared for the real-life experience of a mortar attack, a suicide bomber, or an improvised explosive device (IED). The sense of purpose in the mission may hold some motivation, and the larger task of service to nation may strengthen one's inner resolve.

However, it is likely that the connection and loyalty to those in your unit provides the most powerful influence to remain and fight courageously. The bond of those who fight alongside one another is a deeply held code established during military training that comes into even clearer focus during the real threat of death. Little holds greater meaning than to fight for and with one's unit.

> I found the relationships I developed to be of profound importance. Though we knew that we had to be prepared to die for one another, especially after 9/11/2001, the most meaningful part of those relationships was in the mundane, ordinary tasks of everyday life in uniform. "Smokin' and jokin'" was an integral part of our day, in between formations and work details, which made those more emotionally and morally volatile moments we encountered in war possible. Had we not done the deliberate and unsensational work of building lasting friendships, forged in the lukewarm lives we led between deployments and combat missions, any connections forged in the fires of the hell of war would have been burnt up.
> **Logan Martin Isaac**

Jesus taught, "No one has greater love than this, to lay down one's life for one's friends" (Jn. 15:13). For those of us who hold Jesus at the center of our faith, we must take this statement very seriously. Those who fight to protect their comrades at any cost to their personal safety have lived out Jesus' teaching at a profound level. Their daily sacrificial devotion to one another sustains them in the toughest circumstances.

This teaching can also help us understand and appreciate how the loss of a comrade may generate grief at a profound level and may also induce feelings of self-blame, including intense anger, guilt, and shame. If someone has experienced this most powerful sense of connection, and then circumstances result in the failure to protect and the loss of those most dearly held, the aftermath may be devastating.

Stress and Injury

Being in a war zone, I did many things in those years that I wasn't proud of, and my conscience kicked me around quite a bit. I started to suffer from episodes of depression, and I had an overpowering sense of uselessness. I couldn't seem to be of any use to anyone else. Looking back, I believe I was suffering from PTSD symptoms, but I didn't know anything about that back then. *Al Hendrix*

All of us have experienced stress in some form. Stress affects everyone differently, depending on each person's experience and personality. Most of the time we are able to manage our feelings and thoughts and bounce back. We might be in a grumpy mood for a while, be less communicative or more impatient with those around us, but this is a temporary state of being. Before too long we usually return to our normal condition. The same stressor may bother one person and not another; one person may react one way while another person a different way. But when stress gets to us, we are not our usual selves. We think, feel, and behave in changed ways.

More intense and more prolonged stress can overwhelm our natural systems of coping, leaving us disoriented from our normal ways of behaving and isolating us from those around us. Unlike familiar stressors, with which we have prior experience and the needed knowledge of how to bounce back, intense or prolonged stress overwhelms us because it is beyond our normal coping strategies. Intense or prolonged stress requires the same recovery tools: caring people to listen, space for reflection, religious practices such as prayer that reconnect us to God. However, when stress is more penetrating and unrelenting, these tools are needed in greater quantity and over a greater amount of time. Additionally, when stress overwhelms our coping strategies, we may be less able than usual to reach out and get what we need.

Intense stress has many causes, but for the purposes of understanding the effects of stress, it may be helpful to categorize some of these causes into four of the big sources: life threat, inner exhaustion, loss, and inner conflict. All of these sources are at least possible, if not probable, during military deployment and combat.

Life Threat

This is an endangering of a person's physical safety. This may occur during and following events of violence or threats of violence that provoke terror, helplessness, horror, and shock. There may be many emotions generated by a life threat, but *fear* is probably the most evident.

Inner Exhaustion

Sometimes called "wear and tear," this is an endangering of a person's energy and focus. This may occur when stress accumulates over time without being resolved and without the person being given the necessary time and space to recover. He or she may experience this deep exhaustion physically, emotionally, mentally, and spiritually. Among the many emotions inner exhaustion can bring about, *fatigue* is probably the most evident.

Loss

This is an endangering of a person's attachment to important persons. This may occur during the illness, injury, and/or death of a loved one. It may also occur with the loss of a marriage or other important relationship, missing the birth of one's child or other significant family events, or the death of a beloved pet. Here, too, loss can cause various emotions, but probably the most obvious one is *grief.*

Inner Conflict

This is an endangering of a person's beliefs and trust. This may occur during or following events that conflict with or betray his or her moral or ethical codes. Such events occur during combat, particularly in current military conflicts where it is not always clear who is the enemy. Inner conflict can generate a host of emotions, but *guilt* or *shame* are probably the most apparent.

This is only a beginning of an exploration of these causes of intense stress or the emotions they are prone to produce. In terms of what emotion and related behavior may be most common, consider *anger*. Unlike fear and sadness, anger is a power-rich emotional response that serves to protect the person from vulnerability. When your identity is shaped in certain bounds of societal expectation of masculinity or self-reliance, you are more likely to demonstrate anger and bury fear, sadness, and guilt. As people, we are all meant to experience the full spectrum of emotion. Anger is not the only emotion needed, but unfortunately it may be the only feeling to which someone has access. How can we help each other connect with the full range of emotion available to us as human beings? In some instances, we will need to wade through someone's anger and listen deeply for what may lay beneath it.

These sources of intense stress and their effects may be experienced by service members and family members. A congregation can play a significant role in responding to stressful lived experiences like these, so it is important to be knowledgeable about different sources and their impact.

Think for a moment about religious practices that engage these stressors. Some Christians practice confession or forms of pastoral counseling that set aside space to unburden inner conflict. The Eucharist or Communion table is a rite of restoration and renewal. Prayers of lamentation, both private and public, name our loss and grief, and implore God's presence and comfort. These are only a few examples of the practices Christian traditions have available in responding to the human experience of overwhelming stress.

War Changes a Person

It was totally surreal coming home after deployment. I truly felt like I was on a different planet. Everything was so clean, like shockingly white clean. Bathrooms now seemed huge. The air was so clean. There wasn't the constant smell of burning trash or dust. It was a real adjustment. I don't criticize anyone for not going to war, but when I got back people seemed so involved in themselves and their own interests and didn't seem to care for each other the way we did "over there."
Charlie Conway

Intense experiences of all kinds impact who we are, how we think and feel, and how we behave. Being in the military, being deployed, and seeing combat includes a number of intense experiences. When anyone experiences stress, that person's body generates extraordinary levels of specific biochemicals, such as cortisol, that affect how the person feels emotionally, how his or her body functions physically, and how one's brain works. If the level of stress is overwhelming in degree, either in the level of severity or the prolonged nature of the stress without relief, there may be a lasting change to the way particular parts of the brain function thereafter, even when the person is no longer in a dangerous environment.

> It was the first time I had been in a country gripped by abject poverty; everywhere, there were broken roads, 20-story slums, and blasted-out homes. I brought a lot of that visceral imagery back home with me, and I struggled with that for about three months. *Sarah Schott*

Because the brain is still operating as though stress is present, a person may experience intrusive thoughts, memories, and nightmares, or find it hard to relax or remain calm in certain situations. That person may appear edgy, anxious, or distracted, or seem to have a short attention span. The person may also have a difficult time engaging in a conversation, making commitments, or being in relationship. To those of us on the outside, this person may seem to act strangely and not conform to our expectations. But if our response is to withdraw from that person because he or she isn't acting "right," we may serve to confirm that person's worries and actually make the situation worse.

> In Basic Training, any sense of individuality is torn away and new identities as a group member are put in its place. I don't deny it can save lives in combat, but regaining a meaningful sense of self after those kinds of experiences was made difficult by the degree of commonality that military camaraderie requires. How does one return to being a constructive, self-moderating member of society after spending years and years in such intense service to something bigger than themselves? The loss of meaning either after combat or upon discharge can be

devastating, and finding that balance during and after my service was by far the most difficult for me. ***Logan Martin Isaac***

Individuals dealing with this level of personal change are well aware that they aren't who they used to be, and this may be generating confusion, doubt, and hesitancy in them, particularly when it comes to interpersonal interactions. They may be asking, "If I take the risk to reach out, will I be received or rejected? What if things are going well, but then something triggers me and my behavior scares or shocks those who witness it?" Many veterans may anticipate the discomfort of others, and expect others' passive withdrawal from relationship or even outright rejection. And underneath that anticipation may be the fear that the changes experienced may result in a lifetime of misunderstanding, failed connections, and social isolation.

The few friends who were still around seemed like little children to me. My experience had changed me, and I couldn't identify with them. Vietnam was not a popular war, and their comments about being "baby killers" or other crude names didn't help me at all. I once went into a restaurant where I had eaten for years growing up, and because I had my uniform on, they wouldn't serve me. At various times during this period, I considered exploring religion for myself. I visited several different churches, but I always felt so out of place and awkward that I never went twice to the same one. I moved around a lot in those days. I just felt so out of place. ***Al Hendrix***

Change is an inevitable part of being alive. Our experiences generate change. Intensely stressful experiences may cause more significant change and may create challenges to the process of integrating and growing with those changes. For those of us who believe God's grace is working in this world, strengthening, comforting, and restoring us even in seasons of our lives when we feel distant from God, no experience, no matter how terrible, puts any one of us beyond God's reach. Church communities can be helpful resources to those who have experienced overwhelming stress, including combat experience. We all need a reminder of God's grace sometimes, and every one of us can be that reminder for someone in the way we listen and respond.

Discussion Questions

Personal Reflection:

1. What are my thoughts and feelings about violence, and what personal experiences have shaped that thinking?
2. What are my thoughts and feelings about those who enact violence?
3. When have I experienced intense stress? How did it impact me? What did I do to manage my thoughts and feelings, and get back to my normal mood?
4. When the cause of intense stress was different (life threat, inner exhaustion, loss, or inner conflict), how did it impact me differently? Did I manage it differently? How?

For Small Group Discussion:

Consider sharing your reflections on the questions above. Also, it may be important to reflect on:

1. Has violence impacted our congregation? How did we respond?
2. When members have dealt with intense stress, how has our congregation engaged with them?
3. What religious resources (sacramental or ritual practices, biblical narratives) do we draw on in our tradition that could engage the persons who have experienced intense stress?

4

★ ★ ★

The Life of Military Families

There is an old legend from the warrior society of Sparta. The warrior king, Leonidas, selected three hundred warriors for a mission that would certainly end in their death. He selected warriors, not based on individual skill or strength, nor on their ability to fight together. It was not their courage he was considering, but the courage of their wives and mothers to endure the assured loss. Leonidas knew the nation's fortitude rested on the endurance of its women. The warriors were ready to serve and lay down their lives in honorable battle, but the resolve and resilience of their families would spell the fate of the society.

Today, the story is much the same. Those who serve in uniform receive training to prepare for battle. However, those who serve do not do so as individuals; their service and sacrifice do not belong entirely to them, but to their parents, spouses, children, and all loved ones. The experience of service members directly or indirectly impacts their families.

Our congregations have the great opportunity and responsibility to care for military families both while service members are deployed and upon their return. Military families deal with all the same things any family deals with, but their lives are also different in some significant ways. In order to best engage with these families, we need to know more about their reality.

Unique Opportunities and Challenges

For over 15 years I have sacrificed independence, and a lot of time with my kids and extended family. While my kids were little, I had to work so much that there are many details about their lives I missed or don't remember. Every time I'm gone for over a week, the kids stop doing homework and their grades go down. ***Michelle Hart***

The military is designed to be the most encompassing and demanding institution in American society. It involves the most forceful elements of institutional power: service members and their families are subject to the most sudden and life-altering demands that employment responsibility could entail, 24 hours a day, 7 days a week; personal identity is deeply formed in the culture and ethos of the institution to the extent that it is sometimes hard to tell where the service member ends and the person begins; and one's personal choices and concern for self and family are sacrificed for the higher purpose of defending one's nation.

The military provides its active-duty families with housing support, health care, moving logistics, and a broad range of program resources. The military is total institution: demanding all and providing all. While the service member signs on the dotted line, the whole family is a part of military service in its own way.

Military families, particularly during deployment, go above and beyond to support each other. Spouses comfort, visit, care for each other's children, and share resources to degrees rarely seen elsewhere in American society. This unique kind of community arises from the distinct challenges placed on military families.

Normal military life for families regularly involves some or all these stresses: frequent geographic household relocations; living under the uncertainty created by a family member's job taking precedence over all else, including over illness, the birth of a child, and the needs of the marriage; a highly regimented life that doesn't often foster natural growth in relationships; hearing periodic rumors of harm to or deaths of your loved ones; being detached from mainstream American life; and the lack of personal control over income, job promotion, and other benefits.

Now consider the exceptional challenges that a military family confronts upon deployment. Take a moment to imagine the most stressful and difficult circumstances that can befall a family. At or near the top of the list would likely be separation, illness or incapacitation, and death. Every time a service member deploys, all three of these are brought into the family's awareness in a heightened way: separation for an uncertain amount of time; the threat of illness and loss of physical and/or cognitive capacity; and the threat of loss of life.

Cycles of Deployment

My family was glad to see me when I got back and very welcoming. The military does a pretty good job training families how to prepare for deployments and how to act when their loved one gets home. It is a tough transition, though. **Charlie Conway**

In order to more fully consider the unique challenges facing military families, let's focus on the process of deployment. The deployment cycle is fraught with dynamics with which very few civilian families would be familiar. During the pre-deployment stage, the family is preparing for the departure of their loved one, and may express their anxiety and concern through anger and more frequent confrontations, acting out in other ways, and emotionally withdrawing. Although the family is planning for this departure to be temporary, they may feel the weight of the possibility of permanent departure as well, adding to the difficulty of this transition.

During deployment, the family back home and the service member abroad are both adjusting to this new reality of separation. They may experience loneliness, depression, anxiety, emotional avoidance, and other forms of distancing. The service member is likely deeply occupied with his or her job, working seven days a week, fully immersed in the mission at hand. The family is reorienting the balance of survival in the absence of their loved one. All the tasks of family life still need to be fulfilled, but now without the presence and participation of the service member.

Homecoming usually includes an immediate honeymoon phase of joy and recommitment, followed by a longer—and often challenging—readjustment phase. Roles, responsibilities, and the dynamics of life at home have changed while the service member was deployed, and the reintegration process can be awkward and difficult for all involved.

The service member will be changed by combat experience, and the family will have changed during the service member's absence. The real challenge of reintegration is to recognize, receive, and integrate those big and small changes into one's family. With every change comes the loss of whatever one had to leave behind, and so homecoming involves grief as the family faces the changes. Babies begin to crawl and then walk, have their first laugh and then their first words, and while seeing your child grow up can be cause for celebration and excitement, when a parent misses those notable moments, there is a sense of loss. Service members miss births and birthdays, anniversaries, family members' illnesses and death. There is little time or space to consider the significance of such changes while deployed. During that time of reintegration following deployment, military families need support in setting expectations, communicating their needs, and genuinely processing their grief. Unfortunately, because homecoming is deemed to be a joyful blessing, these real needs for support often go unattended.

> When I was home, as a family, we fell into our normal routines and focused on having fun together, eating, catching up, and generally being who we were. It was refreshing, but I think hearing their fears (theological, personal, political, etc.) would have been an important learning tool for me, to sharpen my own ideas about what is good and right or wrong and ill-advised. **Logan Martin Isaac**

This generation of military service is dealing with a new challenge: multiple deployments. Without a draft, fewer citizens are serving during war and have deployed at record rates. The process of preparation, adjustment, and reintegration is being repeated by some families on a near annual basis. There may be parts of the process that the family becomes more familiar with and become easier over time, but that is not a given. Each member of the family is growing and changing and so are the relationships. The timing and circumstances of one deployment may vary greatly to the next.

The same is true with the experiences and needs wrapped around reintegration.

> My wife was concerned about some of the psychological issues I dealt with. She prayed diligently for me, and she loved me through it. My extended family loved me and supported me but didn't really know what to do with my experiences. ***Patrick Stefan***

Our congregations are made up of families, and we have rich traditions of accompanying persons throughout the whole of their lives, "from cradle to grave." Life can be full of uncertainty, and stress comes along with it. A church community can be a place to share our joys and concerns, receive compassionate care, and seek and receive understanding. It happens through worship, sacramental practices, education, prayer, and sharing meals. Congregations can provide all this and more to our military families, and in the process we will raise stronger, healthier children, nurture more loving marriages, and save lives.

> Congregations can provide care teams, especially if they can involve veterans, and reach out constantly to the families here at home. It may seem silly, but that small gesture of a phone call, email, or just dropping by with a jug of milk or loaf of bread or a casserole means so much to a family that feels lonely and isolated. A consistent, caring, spiritual presence could help prevent a lot of the anxiety and loneliness that can lead to marital problems while the service member is deployed. ***Charlie Conway***

Military families' experience with the ups and downs of deployments, relocations, reunions, and goodbyes are rich gifts for our congregations. Military families have had to learn to be realists, taking on these challenges one day at a time. They can teach our congregations a lot about what is possible and what is needed. They have gone through the very kinds of changes and reorienting process that we need to understand and engage in within our congregations. As a congregation accompanies a service member and military family, they will experience the emotions of deployment and the struggle to adjust to separation, the emotions of reunion and the excitement and process of reintegrating in meaningful ways, and the emotions of knowing this could all happen again with the next redeployment.

Laura Fauntleroy grew up in Texas, one of five children. Her family is filled with ministers in the Christian Church (Disciples of Christ), and the church was a central community in her life as she was growing up. She became a military spouse in 1985 when she married Kyle. Their family, which includes their two children, has experienced three decades of active duty military service and multiple deployments.

> In 2003, the war began again for our family. My husband had deployed during Desert Storm in 1991, several times in between, and now again for Operation Iraqi Freedom. He was on the USS Nimitz, an aircraft carrier, and was going to be in the Persian Gulf for at least nine months. At that point, there was not an end-date to the deployment. Our two children were in middle school.
>
> I have never been so scared in all of my life. Many of our neighbors were deploying with various services and units. For twelve months, I held a letter that a Marine had written for his wife, one of my best friends, and I was to give it to her in the event that he did not return alive. He later deployed again for another year, and I held that sacred letter once again. That was the context of our world.
>
> At times it felt that those of us left behind were simply clinging to each other with this strange intensity and intimacy, trying to help each other breathe, trying to take one step forward together every day until who knew when. We stayed incredibly busy to keep our minds distracted and our bodies exhausted, all the while helping to maintain as much of a normal life as possible for the kids.
>
> We want to be like you, we want to blend in and be "normal," but, especially in times of deployment, we don't feel like we really fit anywhere. At the same time, we want to be strong, to do right by our spouses who are deployed, and handle all of life's tasks all by ourselves, without asking for help. The strength I have witnessed in my fellow military spouses is unbelievable. But we very rarely ask for help. So don't wait for it. Our church families need to take the risk to jump in there. It almost doesn't matter what it is that you do...just that you do something.
>
> One year, my husband's deployment was extended and he was possibly going to miss being home by Christmas. The kids and I were all

making the best of it. We got a tree and decorated it. But our house was the only one on the street without lights.

Then one day I came home from work to find my neighbor in my driveway, climbing down his ladder. He had hung Christmas lights on our house. He didn't ask. He didn't wait for me to ask. He just did it. That one simple act of kindness is one of the greatest gifts I've ever received, even all these years later.

Being there for military families is a complicated endeavor. I wish there was an easy answer, and I wish we could tell you what we need. But many times, we are just breathing and stepping forward. Be present and be involved. Be a Samaritan and hold others' needs as your own. Be observant. Bring a lasagna. Take my kids to the zoo with yours. Meet me for coffee. Show up and hang the lights. Bring fresh plants for the patio. Pick up the dry cleaning. Send a note. Talk to me. Sit and listen to me. Be. Hold. *Laura Fauntleroy*

Discussion Questions

Personal Reflection:

1. As a member of your family, recount times when your family endured a hardship of some kind. How were you affected? How did your family communicate, behave, and change?
2. Who outside your family was able to support you? How were they effective in supporting you during that time?
3. What spiritual practices helped you to process that hardship for yourself?

For Small Group Discussion:

Consider sharing your reflections on the questions above. Also, it may be important to reflect on:

1. How does the cycle of deployment and reintegration experienced by military families inform our process of accompanying military service members and their families?
2. What changes could we make within our congregation that would better address the needs of military families?
3. What if the families in our congregations showed the kind of commitment that military families show each other? What could that look like in our congregation and how might we work toward that end?

5

★ ★ ★

Pastoral Response and the Role of Community

When I got back, I found a new church family near my duty station in Washington that had a lot of veterans. They were really kind and welcoming. They asked questions about my experiences but didn't push for details. They just gave me a chance to talk if I wanted—that was important. I really needed time to decompress, and I took a couple weeks off and travelled around to see people. It is great when people show a genuine interest in you and your experiences but don't push for details and don't treat you too differently, like you are sick or need help.
Charlie Conway

Anyone who has been through intense experiences of violence, loss, and overwhelming stress understands the need for meaningful relationships to process that experience, grow, and become stronger. Without such support, we may remain stuck in our grief, guilt, anger, or sadness, dwelling in a place of despair and depression, without a sense of how to move forward. Military service members and their families who have been through intense experiences will need trustworthy and caring persons to hear their stories and provide the needed support.

Confusion marked my return from combat. I was not depressed or suicidal, but things I used to live for seemed dull and uninspiring. I eventually regained the pleasure I had for those things, but it took a lot of work that the military did not have a part in. I had very strong relationships with several civilians before I went to war, and I returned to those friendships afterward. But without them, I always wonder if I would have adjusted to post-combat life nearly as well as I managed to. Having those relationships bookend the experience of war had the effect of reminding me of who I was before war and who I could be after. **Logan Martin Isaac**

Christian Perspectives on Suffering

Understanding stress, strain, and suffering is not only an emotional capacity but a theological one. There is not a unified Christian theology of suffering. And questions pertaining to evil, sin, and suffering have been among the most divisive in the history of Christian traditions. Just as we explored Christian perspectives on war, we need to explore and become more aware of the different Christian perspectives on suffering. The following views are just a sampling, and usually a given Christian tradition incorporates more than one of these perspectives. I separate them from one another below, however, so we can more readily identify and understand each one.

Suffering as Punishment

In this perspective, suffering is a consequence of sin, a consequence of persons turning away from God. Human suffering is viewed as a punishment for turning away. This is probably the dominant perspective in Christian traditions and seen again and again in the biblical accounts of Adam and Eve, Cain and Abel, Noah and the flood, and so on.

Seeing yourself as responsible for your actions can be important for accountability to self, community, and God, but if this sense of responsibility becomes overwhelming, it is easy to blame yourself and become stuck in a cycle of self-degradation and shame. We are responsible for our choices, but not all circumstances allow for good choices. Such situations can result in survivors' guilt, where the self-condemnation "I should have done more" becomes deeply lodged in our minds, sometimes blocking out compassion, forgiveness, and grace.

Suffering as Redemptive

In this perspective, suffering is also an act of God, not to punish, but to redeem. Suffering is meant to turn us back toward God, or perhaps to turn others back toward God. The biblical image of the suffering servant, first seen in Isaiah 53 and later shaping much of the Christian theology of the crucifixion of Christ, depicts this kind of suffering. Unlike suffering as punishment, redemptive suffering may be undeserved by the one who suffers. Suffering is meant to call out the complicity of others, to invite their repentance, and to evoke a compassionate response toward the one suffering.

Suffering as Injustice

In this perspective, suffering is caused by actions against God's will. These actions that cause the suffering and the suffering itself are beyond the scope of our understanding or rationalization. We look for those responsible and never find them. A person lives a good and healthy life, but dies of illness while suffering intensely. Experiencing confusion and anger against such suffering is also found in the Bible, particularly in the Psalms, Lamentations, and the books of the prophets. In these accounts, persons faithfully call out to God for answers.

This perspective is perhaps the most challenging to accept because it doesn't provide a clear vision of God's plan and our responsibility in our own suffering. This perspective asserts that God neither causes nor desires our suffering, but what of God's power to protect the faithful? This protest is what fuels the protest and lamentations of the Psalms, and many today who faithfully pray for God's intervention.

What Each of Us Believes

Just as our perspective on war impacts our encounter with those who have served in the military, so our perspective on suffering impacts our encounter with another person's experience of suffering. This is further complicated, because the person we are meeting has his or her own perspective on suffering. When we hear other people's stories of suffering, they are sharing both the account of the suffering and how they understand it, and as we listen we are bringing our own understanding. If you want to meet them on their terms and hear their experiences as openly as possible, you will want to be clear about your own perspective and how it may be interacting with those around you.

> Look at the actual needs of the military family. If a service member is away, do their kids need help getting to church? Could they [members of the congregation] take time out to step in and help while the other parent is "single-handedly doing it all"? I've been to churches that looked down upon a family while their spouse was gone and, instead of helping them, badmouthed them for not being in church. Churches should be compassionate and show Christ's love to families and realize it's very difficult to do things by yourself while your spouse is away. The biggest suggestion is just to get to know the family and what specific needs they have. Each family is different. **Michelle Hart**

Theology is not the only source shaping our thinking about the intense experience of combat. A lot of attention is paid to the consequence of stress by frequent media reports of military Post-Traumatic Stress Disorder and incidents of suicide. And while this attention has raised our national concern for the well-being of veterans, it has also painted a picture that doesn't fully portray military experience and those who have served. While it is certainly true and fair to expect that service members and their families have endured some intense stress related to their service to the nation, it is unfair to depict them in a general sense as injured, mentally ill, or suicidal. Often these generalizations, shaped by external sources, go unacknowledged, so it is important to recognize the potential pitfalls of this reality. Rather than focusing on the images drawn by the media or Hollywood, we need to take a radically different approach in responding to service members and their families.

The Church became my new community of meaning; my pastor or priest became my new commanding officer. Those places and people didn't necessarily know this, but I gave them a certain attention and power that had previously been reserved for other military personnel. ***Logan Martin Isaac***

Responding to Strengths

John 3:8 says, "The wind blows where it chooses, and you hear the sound of it, but you do not know where it comes from or where it goes. So it is with everyone who is born of the spirit." And I immediately got it. I was not yet born of the spirit, and my entire life had been an effort to do it all by myself, to try and fly against the wind that runs through all of us and shows us the way. In my own defense, I had no idea that there was a wind of life around me that was always prepared to help. Since I have come to know that fact, I've had no problem feeling that wonderful wind blowing in and around me any time I choose to reach out for it. I know today that I cannot change the wind, but I can adjust my sails such that I can move with the current, and then I don't have to fight to stay in the mainstream of life. I belong here. ***Al Hendrix***

No one wants to be treated like the sum total of their weaknesses, failures, and bad decisions. All of us have those, but we are much more than that. If we pay enough attention we will notice the strengths, successes, and wise decisions that accompany our daily struggles. So how do we respond when we meet a new person? Do we see that person as needing our help, or do we bring a sense of hope for the mutually beneficial potential of that new relationship? This may be important to consider in a general sense with everyone we encounter, but it is particularly important when considering initiating and building relationships with veterans and military families.

If veterans or their family members are treated like victims of their experiences, or as charity cases that you have adopted, their reaction to you will likely be negative. Even when a person is suffering, or in some way out of sorts, it is much easier to receive support that arrives through a mutual, trusting relationship than when the response comes with the condescension of a "handout." Remember that whatever that person is dealing with is less than their value and their strength as a person. Consider that person standing before you to be a survivor and who has found the necessary inner and outer resources to live in spite of challenges, problems, and failures.

> My spiritual life provided a framework for seeking meaning. It has given me the tools needed to understand death and devastation, and it has given me relief for the activities I participated in. My faith has picked me up and carried me through many difficult times and dark thoughts. Studying the Bible gave me purpose and provided me with a productive means of thinking about the new complex and complicated world that I discovered. **Patrick Stefan**

When you look for the resourcefulness in people, it is easy to discover their strength. When you look for their gifts, you may realize ways they can contribute to the well-being and vitality of the community. And when you affirm people's value, you create an opportunity to earn their loyalty and respect, creating a foundation for a lasting and trustworthy relationship.

A Time to Rebuild

> My spiritual life has been absolutely pivotal in processing my military experience. My belief in a Higher Power never wavered, even through the worst of it, and when I think back, this is where I believe I first received my Call to help others and give back the grace that I had found in my dark night of the soul. **Sarah Schott**

Recovery and restoration are a process like tending the house you live in. Picture your sense of self, morality, and spiritual orientation as a house that you live in. That house is the place you come home to and there find comfort and familiarity. When it is storming, that house protects you. The house is made by the formative people and experiences in your life: your family and friends, important teachers and mentors, and your experiences in church growing up. Can you picture your own "house"? Which people or which experiences helped to build it? What is present on the outer walls? What does it feel like inside?

If you have been privileged to have affirming relationships and meaningful experiences, this house is probably well designed, sturdy, and spacious. It is a safe place of comfort and calm. But, realistically, most of us will have some weak spots—maybe a leaky roof, some crumbling dry wall, a sagging foundation.

No matter how well built your house may be, stressful events can shake the house to its foundations. You can blame the building materials or the builder or the deferred maintenance or the magnitude of the earthquake all you like, but sometimes an event just overwhelms this house. How would you feel standing beside your house turned to rubble? Would you feel sad at its loss? Would you feel angry at the storm, or the imperfections and weakness of the house, or yourself for not preventing its downfall? Would you feel embarrassed or ashamed if you looked around and other houses in your neighborhood appeared to be just fine?

What would you do next? Some people will be so devastated by the destruction that they will want to give up altogether. They will look at all that rubble and decide to walk away. Others will get stuck in the hopelessness, not knowing what to do or where to start, or arguing down any potential solution that presents itself. But an amazing opportunity is presented in the aftermath of this destruction. Sticking with the metaphor a bit longer, there is a chance to rebuild.

It is likely that some of the materials from the old house need to be discarded, but others may be useful and need to be incorporated into the new shelter. If you try to only use the old tools and supplies, you will probably fail to construct a better structure and may not even build an adequate one. A person needs to discern what didn't hold up and needs to be replaced. The experience of collapse can help refine the new design and construction efforts.

Processing my military experience in light of my whole life, which included the willingness to die or to kill at the command of another, required a community that embraced me in good times and in bad, in sickness and in health, when I was rich and when I was poor. The military taught me that my life is inseparable from those who surround me, the friends on my left and on my right. **Logan Martin Isaac**

It is necessary to find the needed, new materials and to identify those who can help with the reconstruction efforts. While there may be people ready to help, defining roles is critical. If it's your house, don't have someone else design it or do all the work to build it. That's your responsibility. But that doesn't mean you have to do it all yourself. Find the people who can help with the heavy lifting. Find the people who are specially qualified to work on windows, pipes, electricity, and painting. A community of support is needed to rebuild.

With courage and the necessary support system, this rebuilding process can result in what the clinical field calls "post-traumatic growth." The term is a good reminder to all of us that overwhelming stress and horrific events don't necessarily need to end in a mental health diagnosis. Overwhelming stress and events do not even need to end in despair and hopelessness. Although a lot of work is required by the impacted persons, their families, and their interpersonal support systems, there exists the possibility for greater strength, wisdom, and determination. The house that is rebuilt can be sturdier, more spacious, and a better overall fit than the house that was laid to ruin.

> Processing my experience in the military gradually brought me closer to God. When you are really alone you really need a constant source of strength. I found mine through scripture, study, and prayer.
> **Charlie Conway**

Congregations have the supplies and folks needed for these rebuilding efforts. Look around your church community and see all the expertise that could be put to good use. These resources and helping hands are what our congregations have to offer.

Discussion Questions

Personal Reflection:

1. What do you believe about God's role in human suffering?
2. How might that belief support or impede accompanying a suffering person?
3. In your life, when have you been faced with a rebuilding challenge?
4. What changes did you make during the rebuilding?
5. Who worked with you to support the rebuilding?
6. Have you been able to support someone else in his/her rebuilding project?

For Small Group Discussion:

Consider sharing your reflections on the questions above. Also, it may be important to reflect on

1. What does our congregation believe about God's role in human suffering?
2. How might that belief support or impede accompanying a suffering person?
3. How has our congregation supported the rebuilding efforts of its members in the aftermath of significant life changes (traumatic deaths, loss of job, etc.)?
4. Where does our congregation look for resources within our tradition?

6

★ ★ ★

A Vision of Action

While serving as a chaplain at a VA hospital, I was often asked by those I was visiting if I had served in the military. At that point in time I was a civilian, and I was distracted by the question. There were certain implications imbedded in that question, and I felt I was being dismissed because of my civilian status, even before they knew me as a minister.

I now understand that question—Have you served?—differently than before. It is true that for some it is a question of qualification, and thereby disqualification, depending on the answer. There are service members who have a difficult time trusting and relating to those who have not served in the military. But I have come to believe that in most cases there is greater depth and significance to that question.

First, it is a question that will test your integrity: Will you answer truthfully and confidently? Or will you get frazzled and take offense as I did when I was a civilian? Second, it is a question that will test your resolve and assurance: Will you remain in this conversation with me despite the differences in our respective lived experiences? Or will you tell yourself, "This service member would rather talk to someone else," and thereby remove yourself from the interaction?

Service members have experienced civilians asking questions that they perceive as dumb or insensitive, and so it is understandable that they might proceed with caution. But if that caution turns to avoidance, either by the service member or by the civilian in the conversation, both parties are poorer for it. Service members who can only talk with other service members live in a very small interpersonal universe. And civilians who feel inadequate to listen and respond to the lived experience of service members miss out on the opportunity to engage in learning about an experience that is not their own. In both directions, there is a value in difference and earned mutual respect.

> Each veteran has a different story to tell; there is no such thing as a "normal" military story. A veteran's worth should not be measured by his or her status as honorable, general, uncharacterized, or dishonorable; the military does enough to reinforce shame all on its own, and civilian sources could do a lot of good by being more impartial in granting their support. All veterans deserve respectful response, engagement, and support, regardless of their stories, but it's important that civilians not assume that we've all had similar experiences. Service members join the military for a host of different reasons; we all come from different social locations. We bring our pre-military lives in with us, which often affects our military life, and that can also set the tone for our post-military lives. We are not the sole sum of our military experiences, and we could often use help realizing that. **Sarah Schott**

Each congregation handles differences within its body in its own ways. You may feel more or less comfortable with matters that are unfamiliar. If persons of other races, nationalities, first-languages, age, or sexuality walk through your church's door, do you see these differences as opportunities for learning? Many of us experience discomfort when encountering persons who are different and unfamiliar, and the impulse may be to avoid those differences and thereby lessen our discomfort.

But this manner of avoidance falls short of the example of Jesus' life. As he traveled, taught, and healed, Jesus was eating and drinking with those who were different than him and different than one another (Mt. 9:10; 11:19; Mk. 2:16; Lk. 7:34). Again and again, he invites those of different backgrounds to share a meal together and to nourish themselves, shoulder to shoulder, with those who are different. Our openness and hospitality begins with his example. As Christians, we are challenged to see and celebrate every person in the likeness of God, the same way that Jesus would have.

Authentic work of compassionate care and hospitality can be a little uncomfortable, because it involves taking risks that take us outside our familiar comfort zones. Sometimes providers of pastoral care talk about creating a "safe space," but this notion of safety can't mean that everybody is going to feel *comfortable* all the time. If a person shares his or her experiences with you, he or she is taking a risk to be vulnerable with you. And if you are able to hear this person with compassion and be present to all his or her experiences entail, you are taking a risk to be vulnerable too. Both persons in this interaction need to take that risk so that trusting relationships can be discovered and nurtured. Trust is established through experience, so it's not enough to say, "Hey, you can trust me." Listening and responding compassionately are what builds trust.

A Community of Service

Sometimes people get stuck worrying about their differences and forget the potential for meaningful connection through shared values. As previously discussed, service is often the most commonly shared value of those in the military. Don't our congregations also hold service in high esteem? The commitment to serve ought to be the sort of shared value that brings military folks and church folks together. The leadership qualities instilled during military training and fortified during military service could contribute a great deal to the missions of our congregations. And opportunities to serve the community are likely to appeal to a number of service members and their families.

One of the great community service success stories of this generation is the organization The Mission Continues (www.missioncontinues.org). Their slogan says a lot: "It's not a charity, it's a challenge." The organization "redeploys" veterans to new service opportunities around the country—an engagement of the persistent desire of veterans to serve the good of the nation. The organization features two programs: one that places individual veterans in service leadership positions in the community, and another that teams veterans and civilians together for community service projects.

Although this organization does not have a religious component, it is an instructive model for congregations. What are they doing that couldn't be done by any committed congregation? It provides a useful model for mutuality, trust-building, and service that doesn't treat the veteran merely as a subject of charity.

Personal Gifts Inventory

Before embarking on any specific project or partnerships, two kinds of reflection can illuminate the right path. The first is a personal inventory of our values, beliefs, and experiences like the one recommended at the beginning of the book. The second one examines the gifts we can contribute and the scope of the call to the chosen ministry. Consider these questions:

1. What life experiences have uniquely informed my response to service members and their families?
2. What are my professional talents and spiritual gifts that could serve to support and develop relationships with service members and their families?
3. What do I feel particularly called to in this ministry?

Congregational Gifts Inventory

This second discernment process is also needed at the congregational level. Congregations don't need to be mental health clinics or hospitals or veterans' associations. A congregation needs to be a congregation. Each congregation is uniquely gifted, and while congregations in the same denomination or tradition may share certain cultural and religious values, practices, and language, each congregation has its own personality. It would make little sense to make prescriptive suggestions for what all congregations should do in ministry with service members and their families. The best and most effective result is for each congregation to employ its spiritual gifts, in its location, according to the opportunities presented in the local communities.

1. What are your congregation's unique gifts and resources?
2. What do you do well as a congregation?
3. What do you feel called to do in service with veterans and military families?

Remember the story of Jesus walking along the shore and calling to the fishermen. Jesus didn't ask them to do something they had never done or to become people that they weren't; Jesus called them to be fishers of people—to take their lifelong experience, their knowledge, and their wisdom as fishermen, to shift it in a new way and employ it for the glory of God.

As a congregation, your challenge is to take what you already have, what you already know how to do, and do it in another way by bringing those gifts into service of this ministry opportunity.

The Story of The Church of the Resurrection

The Church of the Resurrection, in the greater Kansas City area, began with a dream to build a congregation that could engage people who were not connected and involved in a church. The church's purpose statement reads simply: "To build a Christian community where nonreligious and nominally religious are becoming deeply committed Christians." The church, founded in 1990, has grown to become the largest United Methodist congregation in the United States.

Members in the church saw a need and an opportunity to more intentionally engage with veterans and military families. At that time, veterans in the congregation did not have a way to identify themselves. And the congregation's programs, which may have served reintegration needs, were not aware of how to best reach out.

So they got to work, intentionally integrating the support of veterans and military families into their programs. They trained members of the church who were themselves veterans to be mentors, capable of caring for others who might be dealing with all manner of challenges. They provided special training for their counseling program. They brought in speakers and facilitated book group discussions. They realized there was a chance to be involved, and they thought broadly about how to bring their resources into the lives of veterans and military families.

The congregation estimated that there were more than a thousand veterans already participating in worship and fellowship opportunities, and saw their increased participation as potentially their greatest resource. Having trained these, mostly Vietnam veterans, as mentors, they expected other veterans and particularly the young ones to show up in droves. They bought into the notion that "if you build it, they will come." There was disappointment when only a few younger veterans came and when they did, it was usually only for a short time.

But that disappointment didn't keep them from picking themselves up and trying again. They designated a retired military officer to aid their outreach. In addition to regular program offerings, such as guest speakers, they began veteran writing workshops that proved to be lively and engaged. They realized there were more partners in this work in the community, so they began working side by side with civic and veteran organizations.

They learned that different generations of veterans had different needs and interests, so they established different groups for Vietnam veterans and younger veterans respectively. Similarly, male and female veterans had different needs, so specialization was important in counseling support, and female veterans were paired with female mentors and counselors. They saw that family members and spouses had a different set of needs than the veterans, so they organized a group of mothers and wives. With each of these groups there were unique perspectives and interests, and so each group was given room to grow into its mission as it emerged.

This is a congregational community larger in membership and deeper in financial resources than most churches. This has made it possible to create and recreate program offerings in this ministry with veterans and military families. It may be a stretch for any other congregation to replicate their programmatic successes, but their experience is not just a story of what money can do. This is story about living up to God's call on their hearts; about doing what they could, doing it with the best intention, effort, and commitment; and about coming up short, feeling disappointment, and continuing to work at it. They didn't start out perfectly, and they're not perfect now, but they are working faithfully at this ministry.

The story of The Church of the Resurrection is shared in the spirit of celebration and inspiration, not as a blueprint. Perhaps the most useful take away from their experience is that the fruits of their ministry did not appear overnight. You may do everything "right" in your community and not have the results you expected. Certainly there are easier ministries to undertake, but ask those actively involved in this work at The Church of the Resurrection and they will tell you that it is important and worthwhile—and that it is saving lives.

What I Have, I Give You

Genuine acceptance and genuine attempts to help, respect, compassion and empowerment mean a lot more than military discounts. *Sarah Schott*

In the book of Acts is a story about Peter and John walking to the temple for worship and encountering a person who remains outside because of his condition. The man outside is begging, pleading for the mercy of passersby, to be noticed and provided for. He is asking for handouts, and he asks Peter and John for their "spare change." Today, our society has a way of making some people into beggars. Just as Peter and John do in this story, refuse to participate in systems of condescension and marginalization. Let's follow their lead and give something far more than mere handouts. Our congregations have God's healing and transforming power, and it can be brought forth through our ministries.

Although Christian traditions practice liturgies differently, our practices of worship and sacrament are rich resources. The liturgical calendar is a cycle that leads us through the narratives of Christ's birth, life and ministry, crucifixion, entombment, and resurrection. These scriptural narratives connect with elements of our lived experiences: expectant waiting, new hope, celebration, new relationships and new work, successes and failures, stress and suffering, abandonment and fear, lamentation, doubt and disbelief, transcendence and awe.

There are examples of communities ritually bringing their warriors home that can inspire our congregations. In Navajo culture the human need for ritual purification after war is engaged by a process called "The Enemy Way." This ritual process acknowledges and engages a kind of inner sickness that is caused by encountering death firsthand. But this is only the first half of the ritual process. "The Blessing Way" ritual follows; it is a process that engages themes of reconnection, healing, harmony, and peace. The need for ritual purification is both individual and communal; right relationship at the personal and interpersonal levels cannot be restored without ritual practice.

> Religious communities should be open to learning from veterans and the experiences of their families. I recall feeling the burden to demonstrate that I "hadn't changed" and a need to reaffirm to religious communities that, while I may be military, I was still "one of them." It is only now that I realize that the difficulty was that I wasn't "one of them" to a certain degree. **Jamie Hawley**

All congregation's ritual practices embody important aspects of lived experience. And although we may theologically conceive of these sacraments differently, they provide the very resources necessary to aid recovery and wellbeing in the midst of life. How does your tradition ritually practice purification and restoration? In many Christian traditions the ritual practices of baptism and communion set aside special space and attention to claim and reconnect our relationship with God and our place in the congregational community. Rituals of memorial create opportunities to remember and celebrate and also grieve a loss.

The people in our communities are a great resource, but our traditions, rituals, and sacred stories are substantive resources too. Consider how your congregation may already have meaningful gifts to offer. Like Peter and John, when you meet someone, think big and creatively about what you have to offer and then give it generously.

Discussion Questions

Personal Gifts Inventory:

1. What life experiences have uniquely informed my response to service members and their families?
2. What are my professional talents and spiritual gifts that could serve to support and develop relationships with service members and their families?
3. What do I feel particularly called to in this ministry?

Congregational Gifts Inventory:

1. What are your congregation's gifts and resources?
2. What do you do well as a congregation?
3. What do you feel particularly called to action around?

Final Reflections:

1. What have been your most meaningful "learnings" from this book?
2. Where do you see your next step in this ministry?
3. How could you involve your congregation?

Contributors

A number of service members, from different branches of the military and different generations, have contributed to this book with parts of their personal stories and experiences. You will find their voices shared at various times in the proceeding chapters; their comments are set off in boxes. Their experiences and perspectives are different from each other, but each of them shares the hope, as I do, that the church can realize a more engaged connection with service members and their families. Their names and biographical sketches are below.

CHARLES M. CONWAY III grew up in Jacksonville, Florida. He served twenty-six years as a Navy intelligence officer, 1987-2013, attaining the rank of O6. He deployed oversees multiple times, including to Afghanistan. He is a member of the Presbyterian church and currently a student at Iliff School of Theology.

KENT DRESCHER, PH.D., was born in Utah and has lived for many years in San Jose, California. He is married and has two grown sons. Prior to his doctoral training at Fuller Graduate School of Psychology, he received an M.Div. degree from San Francisco Theological Seminary, was ordained by the Presbyterian Church USA, and served as a parish minister for several years. He has worked with combat veterans with PTSD since 1990. He currently serves as Clinical Director for The Pathway Home (www.thepathwayhome.org), a nonprofit, nongovernmental residential PTSD treatment program in Yountville, California. The program provides services exclusively for veterans and active-duty service members who were deployed to the wars in Iraq and Afghanistan and who have struggled with the transition back to civilian life.

LAURA FAUNTLEROY grew up in Dumas, Texas, with four brothers and sisters. She grew up in the Christian Church (Disciples of Christ), and her family is filled with Disciples ministers, including her husband, Kyle; sister Dani and her husband, David; brother, Barry; stepfather, Byron Lamun; and nieces, Douglass Anne and Amber. Laura became a military spouse when she married her husband, Kyle, in 1985. For three decades, Laura, has been involved in supporting military families, including most recently as the instructor of the "Spouse Academy" at the Naval Chaplain School and Center where her husband served as the Commanding Officer (2011-2014). She is the mother of two grown children, Griffin and Grace.

SARAH SCHOTT grew up mostly in Pennsylvania and Georgia. She enlisted in the Navy in 2003, serving three years as a broadcast journalist, and then reenlisted in Army National Guard, serving another four years as a chaplain assistant. Currently she is working as a librarian for the Florida Department of Corrections and pursuing her M.Div. at Iliff School of Theology. She is a member of the United Church of Christ.

MICHELE M. HART grew up in Maple Grove, Minnesota. She enlisted in the Navy in 1998, and has served the last sixteen years with sailors and Marines as a medical corpsman, currently holding the rank of Chief Petty Officer. She attends an Assemblies of God church near where she is currently stationed at Buckley Air Force Base, in Aurora, Colorado.

REV. JAMIE D. HAWLEY, M.DIV., grew up in Gladewater, Texas. He served in the Navy, 1993-2001, in aviation maintenance, attaining the rank of E5. He deployed with the USS Kitty Hawk and USS Carl Vinson. Rev. Hawley is a graduate of Chicago Theological Seminary and ordained in the United Church of Christ. He is currently serving as a chaplain at the University of Michigan Health System in Ann Arbor, Michigan, and pursuing a second graduate degree.

AL HENDRIX grew up in Laramie, Wyoming, and Kansas City. He enlisted in the Navy in 1968, and served nine years as a cryptographer, including four tours in Vietnam, attaining the rank of E7. He attends Camas Friends Church in Camas, Washington.

LOGAN MARTIN ISAAC grew up in Orange County, California. He enlisted in the Army in 2000, and served for six years as a forward observer, attaining the rank of E5. He deployed to Iraq in 2004 as a part of Operation Iraqi Freedom. He is a member of the Episcopal Church and is currently studying theology at the University of St. Andrews in Scotland. He is the author of two books (as Logan Mehl-Laituri); *Reborn on the Fourth of July: The Challenge of Faith, Patriotism, and Conscience* (InterVarsity, 2012) and *For God and Country (in that order): Faith & Service for Ordinary Radicals* (Herald, 2013).

ERIC MOON grew up in Brownwood, Texas, and Ogden, Utah. He enlisted in the Army in 1967 and served three years, including two tours in Vietnam. He currently lives in Berkeley, California, and has worked for the American Friends Service Committee for nearly three decades. He is a member of the Religious Society of Friends (Quakers) and is the father of the author.

BENJAMIN PETERS grew up in Napavine, Washington. He enlisted in the Marines shortly after September 11, 2001, and served for eight years as an imagery analyst, attaining the rank of E5. Although he was a Reservist during that eight years, he deployed twice to Iraq, with tours in 2002 and 2004-2005. Following his military service, he received a M.A. degree from Denver Seminary and is now pursuing a Ph.D. at Iliff School of Theology. He is the author of *Through All the Plain* (Cascade, 2014).

PATRICK G. STEFAN grew up in Big Bear Lake, California. He enlisted in the Marines in 2001 and served ten years as a motor transportation operator, attaining the rank of E6. He deployed to Iraq, in 2003, as a part of the initial invasion of Operation Iraqi Freedom. He continues to serve in the military, currently as a chaplain in the Army (2012-), now holding the rank of O3. He also serves as the Head Pastor of the Rochester Reformed Presbyterian Church in Rochester, New York.

The writer of the Foreword is REV. DR. RITA NAKASHIMA BROCK, Research Professor of Theology and Culture, and Founding Codirector of the Soul Repair Center at Brite Divinity School.

A noted theologian, she has lectured worldwide. In her two years leading the Soul Repair Center, Dr. Brock has become an internationally recognized expert on the emerging study of moral injury and recovery. She is a commissioned minister of the Christian Church (Disciples of Christ) and has served in a number of prominent leadership positions, including being the first chair of the Common Global Ministries Board of the Christian Church (Disciples of Christ) and the United Church of Christ. Her book, coauthored with Rebecca Ann Parker, *Saving Paradise: How Christianity Traded Love of This World for Crucifixion and Empire* was a finalist for an American Academy of Religion Award in reflective, constructive theological studies, and *Publisher's Weekly* selected it as a best book in religion in 2008. In December 2008, she and Dr. Gabriella Lettini began work on the Truth Commission on Conscience in War (www.conscienceinwar.org), which, in November 2010, recommended extensive public education on moral injury. In response, she and Dr. Lettini coauthored *Soul Repair: Recovery from Moral Injury After War* (Beacon, 2012).

Bible Reflections

Reflection on Acts 10:1–23

by Zachary Moon

Acts 10:1–23

In Caesarea there was a man named Cornelius, a centurion of the Italian Cohort, as it was called. He was a devout man who feared God with all his household; he gave alms generously to the people and prayed constantly to God. One afternoon at about three o'clock he had a vision in which he clearly saw an angel of God coming in and saying to him, "Cornelius." He stared at him in terror and said, "What is it, Lord?" He answered, "Your prayers and your alms have ascended as a memorial before God. Now send men to Joppa for a certain Simon who is called Peter; he is lodging with Simon, a tanner, whose house is by the seaside." When the angel who spoke to him had left, he called two of his slaves and a devout soldier from the ranks of those who served him, and after telling them everything, he sent them to Joppa.

About noon the next day, as they were on their journey and approaching the city, Peter went up on the roof to pray. He became hungry and wanted something to eat; and while it was being prepared, he fell into a trance. He saw the heaven opened and something like a large sheet coming down, being lowered to the ground by its four corners. In it were all kinds of four-footed creatures and reptiles and birds of the air. Then he heard a voice saying, "Get up, Peter; kill and eat." But Peter said, "By no means, Lord; for I have never eaten anything that is profane or unclean." The voice said to him again, a second time, "What God has made clean, you must not call profane." This happened three times, and the thing was suddenly taken up to heaven.

Now while Peter was greatly puzzled about what to make of the vision that he had seen, suddenly the men sent by Cornelius appeared. They were asking for Simon's house and were standing by the gate. They called out to ask whether Simon, who was called Peter, was staying there. While Peter was still thinking about the vision, the Spirit said to him, "Look, three men are searching for you. Now get up, go down, and go with them without hesitation; for I have sent them." So Peter went down to the men and said, "I am the one you are looking for; what is the reason for your coming?" They answered, "Cornelius, a centurion, an upright and God-fearing man, who is well spoken of by the whole Jewish nation, was directed by a holy angel to send for you to come to his house and to hear what you have to say." So Peter invited them in and gave them lodging.

This kind of story may seem familiar in this part of the Bible: Jesus or the disciples meeting up with some person and sharing fellowship. But if we look at the cultural context of this meeting, we will appreciate just how unlikely and risky this meeting would have been. Peter was a part of a community at odds with the Roman military and the likes of Cornelius. In the presence of a centurion, Peter would have likely been very uncomfortable, even fearful. He didn't know Cornelius personally, but he would have perceived the many differences in their worldview and experiences.

This story may also be familiar because it is like so many "call narratives" in the Bible: God calling someone to deepen their faith and live it out in the world, only to see that chosen person argue in all kinds of ways that God has somehow made a mistake in making such an invitation. Remember Moses and the burning bush? Moses sounded more like a skillful attorney conducting his best rebuttal than a grateful and willing servant.

But stories such as these are a precious gift to us today. As we read these stories of others' faithfulness and resistance, these stories challenge our faithfulness in terms in which we can understand and relate. Sometimes saying "yes" to God's invitations is difficult, and we may seek to renegotiate the offer to make things a little easier. For Cornelius and Peter to get together, both needed to overcome some barriers and become more open to God moving among them.

We read in the story that Cornelius has a serious relationship with God; although professionally, Cornelius would have needed to display his devotion to Rome. Perhaps God perceives that Cornelius is isolated and in need of community, and so God sends Cornelius toward Peter so that he can benefit from a sustaining relationship in his company, but Cornelius was taking some risks to take this action.

He was doing something that didn't fit smoothly into his cultural framework. And what if Peter didn't meet him halfway? What if Cornelius took the risk and found Peter too different, too fearful, or even just too occupied?

When we read Peter's side, we understand that this meeting nearly fell apart before it began. In the story, Peter has a vision of bounty and nourishment, and he can't turn it all away quickly enough in disgust. His bold resistance demands our attention. Even though Peter recognizes this vision is from God, Peter begins to deny it on religious grounds, saying, "I have never eaten anything that is profane or unclean." Peter is hungry and his vision portrays God providing sustenance, but it doesn't meet Peter's expectations and criteria for what is acceptable.

Yet this story shows God as making no mistake, answering Peter's refusal with, "What God has made clean, you must not call profane." Peter can't comprehend this. He has dedicated his whole life to a certain religious identity, and now it seems as if God is changing the rules. The story says Peter repeated his argument a second and third time, and still didn't entirely get the point until the opportunity to meet with Cornelius presents itself upon his waking from the vision.

This story reveals God as reauthoring the rule book, reminding Peter and all who hear the story that God's mission and purposes are bigger than any of our certainties, religious or otherwise. The story depicts God as intervening because Peter would not be able to respond to Cornelius and enter into relationship with him due to his preconceived notions of who Cornelius was. Here God's role is to bring these two persons together despite the cultural divisions of their time. There was something that needed to take place in and through that encounter. Cornelius and Peter both showed courage in taking risks to be open to that relationship coming about, and they were changed and grew in faith.

Today, do we carry such barriers in our religious tradition or in our personal religious or political thinking that would keep us from being open to having a purposeful and transformative relationship with military service members or their families?

The work of relationship begins with us, just as it does in this text from Acts. Even now, we might experience God as preparing us for relationship with those who may have different experiences and perspectives, and challenging us to rethink our inner, embedded barriers.

If we are oriented in certain political and religious ways, we might think all war, or certain wars, are not justifiable. This may distract us when we meet a service member who has fought in war, and we may be occupied with whether war is justifiable instead of really meeting and engaging with the person standing before us. Likewise, if we are oriented in other political and religious ways in which we see war as necessary to our national defense and American way of life, we could be hung up if a veteran or his or her family member says something about war that doesn't fit with our values and beliefs. We may unintentionally find ourselves stuck just like Peter was—in a way of thinking and believing that renders some folks outside our scope of relationship.

This is the first step in this God-purposed encounter coming into being: we need to get clear with ourselves about our barriers to relationship, be they judgments, beliefs, values, or political positions. That's what getting ready looks like when you feel called to be in relationship with someone different enough than you to raise some of this tension. We have to be willing to say, "All right, God, I won't call profane what you have made clean." And when we awaken from that moment of faithful acceptance, we can meet that person, welcome him or her in, and say as Peter does, "I am the one you are looking for."

Reflection on Romans 12:14—13:7

by Benjamin John Peters

BENJAMIN JOHN PETERS grew up in the Pacific Northwest. He served eight years in the Marines and deployed twice to Iraq as an imagery analyst. He is now pursuing a Ph.D. at Iliff School of Theology and is the author of *Through All the Plain* (Cascade, 2014).

Romans 12:14—13:7

Bless those who persecute you; bless and do not curse them. Rejoice with those who rejoice, weep with those who weep. Live in harmony with one another; do not be haughty, but associate with the lowly; do not claim to be wiser than you are. Do not repay anyone evil for evil, but take thought for what is noble in the sight of all. If it is possible, so far as it depends on you, live peaceably with all. Beloved, never avenge yourselves, but leave room for the wrath of God; for it is written, "Vengeance is mine, I will repay, says the Lord." No, "if your enemies are hungry, feed them; if they are thirsty, give them something to drink; for by doing this you will heap burning coals on their heads." Do not be overcome by evil, but overcome evil with good.

Let every person be subject to the governing authorities; for there is no authority except from God, and those authorities that exist have been instituted by God. Therefore whoever resists authority resists what God has appointed, and those who resist will incur judgment. For rulers are not a terror to good conduct, but to bad. Do you wish to have no fear of the authority? Then do what is good, and you will receive its approval; for it is God's servant for your good. But if you do what is wrong, you should be afraid, for the authority does not bear the sword in vain! It is the servant of God to execute wrath on the wrongdoer. Therefore one must be subject, not only because of wrath but also because of conscience. For the same reason you also pay taxes, for the authorities are God's servants, busy with this very thing. Pay to all what is due them—taxes to whom taxes are due, revenue to whom revenue is due, respect to whom respect is due, honor to whom honor is due.

We live in stories. Our days are marked by the fragmented episodes of a much larger narrative. Yet only in rare, privileged moments do we grasp the whole. The fragments are damning, the arcs redemptive. Trotting the dusty byways of the Mediterranean, Paul moved through history with a story to live out and share. So often, however, we read Paul's epistles as ancient fragments, forgetting the narrative backdrop from whence they came. We forget the story behind the text. Likewise, we frequently encounter the veteran and overlook the person; we see the uniform, but neglect the story. And if by some rare insight, we actually see, we all too often project our sense of what a warfighter should or should not be onto the veteran. Engaging a text, then, is much like encountering a veteran: both require space and sensitivity and a willingness to hear and learn the back story in order to speak.

Paul was writing to the budding Christian communities in Rome with a twofold purpose: one, to introduce himself—he hadn't yet visited the capital—while defending his apostolic credentials; and two, to solidify the identity of the Roman communities, which were comprised of both Jewish and Gentile Christians. He wanted to point out that, though the two groups were culturally different, they held Christ in common, a Christ who could seal their disparate identities.

There's something else, however, lingering beneath the text. Paul was well aware of both the whims of empire *and* the budding revolution in Judea. He knew that at any moment that which he strove for could be undone. Bless those who persecute, live at peace, pay your taxes, and give respect its due was less about living in community or rightly under authority as it was about engaging both the community and society through the narrative of Jesus' reconciling work.

These bits and pieces of Paul are easy. It's the placing of Paul in context and wrestling with his meaning that's difficult. Throughout history this section of Romans (12:14—13:7) has been used to both uphold a Christian pacifism *and* sanction war. On the one hand, there are Christians who claim that we are to live at peace with all people while overcoming evil with good. On the other, there are Christians who claim that the authorities are divinely appointed and that it's the Christian's duty to obey, even unto war. The believing veteran, returning from deployment, is often caught in the mire betwixt these two textual options—both of which *can* be argued as "orthodox." It is a haunting tension. And when a veteran is most in need of a narrative to make sense of her experiences, she is left with fragments, muted shards leading to exegetical confusion.

I was no different. I yearned for an answer to the question that I had posed in Iraq: Was I justified in what I did? And after, I desperately sought a narrative that could both order my history and provide meaning to violence.

"If it is possible, so far as it depends on you, live peaceably with all." But I had killed. Was I then peaceful?

"If your enemies are hungry, feed them; if they are thirsty, give them something to drink." But I had given my enemies bombs and bullets. Did I act in a way that showed I cared about my enemies?

"Let every person be subject to the governing authorities." But I had only followed orders. Was I then justified?

"It is the servant of God to execute wrath on the wrongdoer." But I had despised my actions. Was I then God's servant?

Perhaps there are no right answers. Perhaps all we have are doubts, ambiguities, and deserts of gray. Perhaps all we have is the choice between two textual options: embodied peacemaking *or* justice through war.

Surveying my postwar fragments, I chose the former narrative. For me, Paul was chronicling the active embodiment of God's reconciling work in the world. "Christians," I envisioned Paul as saying, "are to pursue redeeming actions for the purpose of reconciliation. They do not repay evil with evil; rather they respond to evil with acts of love." Yes, the human condition is steeped in sin and death. But, wrestling with Paul, the only sense that I could make, the only healing narrative to be found, maintained that violence didn't redeem, rather it corrupted. It was the antithesis of hope. It was *disbelief*. If Paul was claiming that reconciliation rooted in love could and would transform creation, then I had found a narrative in which to place my fragments, a narrative overflowing with hope.

Every veteran, however, responds differently. My experiences with the United States Marine Corps in the Al Anbar Province are not those of a soldier's in Baghdad or an airwoman's in Qatar. Where

I returned emboldened to navigate postwar ambiguity through the narrative of Christian peacemaking, others came home itching to redeploy. My response wasn't necessarily normative, but neither was the veteran's currently on his or her sixth or seventh tour.

As congregations seek to construct a coherent narrative out of the fragmented realities of their members, what is it to do with ambiguous exegetical options and those veterans who experience moments of confusion, grief, and pain after returning from combat zones? It recalls Paul's second purpose. No matter what the experience, political persuasion, or religious belief, there is a crucified and resurrected Christ, a narrative that transcends, unifies, and heals. By engaging the human, not the uniform; by asking questions and allowing for anger; by providing a safe space for veterans to process their journeys, the church embodies the story behind the text, the narrative comprised of countless fragments. As Paul writes, "Rejoice with those who rejoice, weep with those who weep." The church succeeds by entering into the humanity of its veterans while validating their process.

Regardless of how I interpret Paul's letter to the Romans, I still wrestle with my role in the United States Marine Corps, Operation Iraqi Freedom, and the church. I remain sitting when veterans are asked to stand and be recognized on those twice-a-year Sundays. I pretend I'm something other than what I am. And yet, each time, I'm reminded: there is a cost to war that outpaces Washington budgets. I don't have the answers. I haven't *finished* the process of collecting my fragments into a cohesive narrative that makes sense of and orders my experiences. I still don't comprehend violence, whether committed or received. I'm neither warrior nor hero. I'm only a veteran struggling to understand the war that made him, and the place that it fits within the larger Christian narrative of both reconciliation and redemption. After all, I live in stories. And stories, when collected and shared, can offer possibilities for healing.

Reflection on Luke 7:2–9

by Logan Martin Isaac

LOGAN MARTIN ISAAC grew up in southern California. He served in the Army for six years and deployed to Iraq in 2004. He is the author of two books (as Logan Mehl-Laituri); *Reborn on the Fourth of July: The Challenge of Faith, Patriotism, and Conscience* (InterVarsity, 2012) and *For God and Country* (in that order): Faith & Service for Ordinary Radicals (Herald, 2013).

Luke 7:2–9

A centurion there had a slave whom he valued highly, and who was ill and close to death. When he heard about Jesus, he sent some Jewish elders to him, asking him to come and heal his slave. When they came to Jesus, they appealed to him earnestly, saying, "He is worthy of having you do this for him, for he loves our people, and it is he who built our synagogue for us." And Jesus went with them, but when he was not far from the house, the centurion sent friends to say to him, "Lord, do not trouble yourself, for I am not worthy to have you come under my roof; therefore I did not presume to come to you. But only speak the word, and let my servant be healed. For I also am a man set under authority, with soldiers under me; and I say to one, 'Go,' and he goes, and to another, 'Come,' and he comes, and to my slave, 'Do this,' and the slave does it." When Jesus heard this he was amazed at him, and turning to the crowd that followed him, he said, "I tell you, not even in Israel have I found such faith."

The centurion had heard about a local healer who could work miracles. He had been told that a few of his men had stolen away one day to witness an odd Jewish ceremony at the Jordan River. The legionaries even claimed to have heard a voice from the clouds call the man "son," a sacrilegious claim. A camelskin-clad Jew had instructed them not to lie or steal, not to grasp at prestige or cut people down in pursuit of rank. Though the charge of absenteeism and blasphemy was harsh, the centurion gave them a slap on the wrist, since it seemed the lunatic had spoken a word of sense to them.

The centurion cared for his men more than other commanders; he called his subordinates "brother" and his servants "son." He made sure his soldiers ate their fill before he would serve himself.

This healer he'd heard of was an oddity. All he knew was that the man touched the sick and did not succumb to the lesions marking their faces. He could not escape the stories circulating about this man, Jesus—particularly lately, since one of his servants had taken ill, and death seemed imminent. He had ordered men left and right; he told some "come" and they came, and others "go" and they went. But he could not order away the demon that possessed his favored servant, the one that was causing the sickness. Maybe this Jesus was a good man like he was; maybe he could bring healing to the centurion's house.

He learned that Jesus would be passing through the area where his unit was stationed. He would try to procure healing for his servant, but he felt awkward. He would go to Jesus without the protection and esteem his military uniform provided. He would be just another man in the crowd.

The crowd was even worse than he expected. Jesus was in the middle of a large throng coming from Capernaum. The centurion hustled to keep up with the crowd, poking his head above the mass, waiting for the best time to try to get closer. How would he address him? Other centurions might hear him if he called out, "Lord, Lord," and report him to others, perhaps gaining favor from their superiors for pointing out his treasonous titling—only Caesar could be Lord. But the crowd was growing; he might not get any other chance. He didn't have time to go back and forth. He cupped his hands around his mouth and shouted as loud as he could:

"LORD! I am not worthy to receive you, but ..."
"... only say the word, and my servant shall be healed."

A war-weary captain sat in the back of the church, his chest quaking with a mixture of guilt and post-traumatic stress disorder (PTSD). He hadn't been to church in many years, not since his first deployment to the Middle East. He had been a devout churchgoer, but the Church had been ill-equipped to exorcise the demons of war he carried back with him. Years ago, in the confessional, he had spoken of what he had seen and done. The awkward pause was heartbreaking, and the stammered response did nothing to put the pieces back together.

He couldn't be sure why he came back after all these years. Entering the church, he instinctively went to cross himself at the font, but staring back at him from the holy water was the image of the publican in Luke 18, another public servant who found little respite from the harrowing of a conscience too-late crystallized. Like Pilate, he couldn't wash the blood from his hands, no matter how hard he tried. His soul was tormented, ripped between faith and service. He fell so short of one and had so excelled at the other.

He had numerous combat decorations. Citations sang his praises for deeds he'd done overseas. Every one of his men came home; not one had been killed in the many deployments he oversaw. His men were like family, and he defended them vigorously. He had even gone the extra mile of learning Arabic and Pashto, so the locals knew they could trust him. But he had to make sacrifices he regretted, and those regrets wracked his dreams most nights.

The time away from home had taken its toll. He was divorced and had lost custody of his children. Others in his unit fared even worse. One sergeant was referred to the behavioral health unit; another attempted suicide three times before he finally got it right. Some of his men got into car wrecks or started on drugs. Maybe there were spiritual stowaways they wrestled with too; he couldn't be sure. Trying to reconnect with them was too hard. It had been years between conversations with some of them.

Watching from the back of the church, he wrestled with whether to go forward for Eucharist. Something held him back, but something else beckoned him forward. The voice of the publican echoed in his ears: "God have mercy on me, a sinner!" (Lk. 18:13, NIV). It was all he could hear some days. Would the Church express the soft, still whisper of God, or the deafening thunderclap of despair?

Reflection on 2 Corinthians 1:1–11

by Kent Drescher

KENT DRESCHER, PH.D. Prior to his doctoral training at Fuller
Graduate School of Psychology, he received a M.Div. degree
from San Francisco Theological Seminary, was ordained by
the Presbyterian Church USA, and served as a parish minister
for several years. He has worked with combat veterans with
PTSD since 1990 and currently serves as clinical director for
The Pathway Home, which provides services for veterans and
active-duty service members who were deployed to the wars
in Iraq and Afghanistan and who have struggled with the
transition back to civilian life.

2 Corinthians 1:1–11

Paul, an apostle of Christ Jesus by the will of God, and Timothy our
brother,

To the church of God in Corinth, together with all his holy people
throughout Achaia:

Grace and peace to you from God our Father and the Lord Jesus Christ.

Praise be to the God and Father of our Lord Jesus Christ, the Father
of compassion and the God of all comfort, who comforts us in all our
troubles, so that we can comfort those in any trouble with the comfort
we ourselves receive from God. For just as we share abundantly in the
sufferings of Christ, so also our comfort abounds through Christ. If we are
distressed, it is for your comfort and salvation; if we are comforted, it is
for your comfort, which produces in you patient endurance of the same
sufferings we suffer. And our hope for you is firm, because we know that
just as you share in our sufferings, so also you share in our comfort.

We do not want you to be uninformed, brothers and sisters, about
the troubles we experienced in the province of Asia. We were under great
pressure, far beyond our ability to endure, so that we despaired of life itself.
Indeed, we felt we had received the sentence of death. But this happened
that we might not rely on ourselves but on God, who raises the dead. He
has delivered us from such a deadly peril, and he will deliver us again.
On him we have set our hope that he will continue to deliver us, as you

help us by your prayers. Then many will give thanks on our behalf for the gracious favor granted us in answer to the prayers of many. (NIV)

Paul's familiar opening to this second letter to the churches in Corinth—"Grace and peace to you from God our Father and the Lord Jesus Christ"—stands in direct contrast to the Roman Empire's Pax Romana (i.e., Roman peace) that was brutally enforced through military might by the Emperor. Paul offers praise to God as the Father of compassion and the God of all comfort. Comfort is offered to God's people so they might provide similar compassion and comfort to others during times of suffering. Compassionate service freely offered to all is to characterize the community of faith that makes up God's kingdom. God's people are not protected from suffering; rather, they are comforted by God and by one another in the midst of suffering.

Paul continues by describing his own recent experience of intense suffering that he says occurred in the province of Asia (present-day Turkey). Scholars disagree as to the exact nature of the suffering experiences Paul describes here. It may have been an illness that nearly caused his death. It may have been some experience of persecution or imprisonment. Later in this letter, Paul makes reference to his famous "thorn in the flesh" (12:7) that some have suggested was a medical condition, such as recurrent malaria, that made him weak at times. He also states, "Three times I was beaten with rods, once I was pelted with stones, three times I was shipwrecked, I spent a night and a day in the open sea" (11:25 NIV). What we know from this opening passage to the letter is that in this particular instance his suffering was overwhelming. He states it was beyond his ability to endure, that he despaired of life, and that he believed he had received a death sentence. Clearly, whatever happened, it was a "dark night of the soul" for Paul. Fear, life threat, hopelessness, and despair come through clearly from his words.

I am struck as I read how similar has been the experience of many of our nation's combat veterans who have endured long months and sometimes years, during deployment and afterward, serving faithfully in harsh and dangerous conditions, during more than a decade of what the military has come to call "the Long War" in Afghanistan and Iraq. Many returning veterans carry in their bodies, minds, and spirits injuries, both physical and emotional, visible and invisible. I have heard numerous veterans tell me in very similar words the pressures of deployment, their feelings of being completely overwhelmed by powerful emotions of grief, fear, or despair, and by some of a powerful sense of foreboding that they might not survive.

Over two million men and women have served our nation over the past decade by deploying to the wars in Iraq and Afghanistan. They are the few in our nation who have an accurate perspective on the human costs and consequences of modern war, but whose voices are mostly silent. Our nation's veterans have been trained to be proud, resilient, and self-sufficient. Most return home from deployment changed but still resilient. However, a subset return home burdened with the emotional costs of war. Perhaps as many as one out of four return troubled by chronic pain, post-traumatic stress, traumatic brain injury, addiction problems, or depression and suicidal thoughts.

Recently, the term "moral injury" has emerged as a new descriptor of the experience of some returning veterans. Combat-related moral injury is not a psychiatric disorder; rather it is a term that reflects the fact that some service members were called upon in the course of their duties to inflict immense devastation with powerful weapons resulting in injury and death within the close confines of civilian cities and villages. For many of those veterans, though fear of dying was an element of trauma, the burden of exposure to violence and inflicting harm is even more consequential.

Our culture continues to have a stigma associated with seeking mental health care. This stigma is also found among our nation's military service members, and, consequently, many veterans suffer silently, in isolation, reticent to ask for help. Many of those returning from Iraq and Afghanistan have unique and individual transition challenges whether they have a mental health problem or not. Many experience financial strain, family stress, problems with returning to the workplace, difficulty getting needed services, even difficulty simply being around one's children. All of these things can make the transition back home difficult.

In his first letter to the churches in Corinth, Paul described the church as a human body, with members functioning together with differing abilities, responsibilities, and roles. Modern science is teaching us that human health and flourishing does not come to "couch potatoes." Health comes from actively moving about in the world and engaging in the lives of others. Extending Paul's metaphor, the health of the Body of Christ is not aided by pew-sitting. Rather, God calls the church to leave the safety of sanctuary walls and enter the world, bringing the compassion and comfort that we have received from God to all those in need in the midst of their pain and suffering.

Ministry to our nation's veterans and service members will not happen by waiting until they come to our buildings. The Body of Christ must rise up, walk, and meet them where they are—in schools, jobs, hospitals, and on the streets. Only through personal encounter can the church design ministry tailored to their specific needs. How will you and your congregation respond to the human suffering that is all around?

Reflection on Luke 15:11–32

by Eric Moon

ERIC MOON enlisted in the Army in 1967 and served three years, including eighteen months in Vietnam. He has worked for the American Friends Service Committee for more than two decades and is a member of the Religious Society of Friends (Quakers).

Luke 15:11–32

Jesus continued: "There was a man who had two sons. The younger one said to his father, 'Father, give me my share of the estate.' So he divided his property between them. "Not long after that, the younger son got together all he had, set off for a distant country and there squandered his wealth in wild living. After he had spent everything, there was a severe famine in that whole country, and he began to be in need. So he went and hired himself out to a citizen of that country, who sent him to his fields to feed pigs. He longed to fill his stomach with the pods that the pigs were eating, but no one gave him anything. "When he came to his senses, he said, 'How many of my father's hired servants have food to spare, and here I am starving to death! I will set out and go back to my father and say to him: Father, I have sinned against heaven and against you. I am no longer worthy to be called your son; make me like one of your hired servants.' So he got up and went to his father. "But while he was still a long way off, his father saw him and was filled with compassion for him; he ran to his son, threw his arms around him and kissed him. "The son said to him, 'Father, I have sinned against heaven and against you. I am no longer worthy to be called your son.' "But the father said to his servants, 'Quick! Bring the best robe and put it on him. Put a ring on his finger and sandals on his feet. Bring the fattened calf and kill it. Let's have a feast and celebrate. For this son of mine was dead and is alive again; he was lost and is found.' So they began to celebrate. "Meanwhile, the older son was in the field. When he came near the house, he heard music and dancing. So he called one of the servants and asked him what was going on. 'Your brother has come,' he replied, 'and your father has killed the fattened calf because he has him back safe and sound.' "The older brother became angry and refused to go in. So his father went out and pleaded with him. But he answered his father, 'Look!

All these years I've been slaving for you and never disobeyed your orders. Yet you never gave me even a young goat so I could celebrate with my friends. But when this son of yours who has squandered your property with prostitutes comes home, you kill the fattened calf for him!' "'My son,' the father said, 'you are always with me, and everything I have is yours. But we had to celebrate and be glad, because this brother of yours was dead and is alive again; he was lost and is found.'"(niv)

There is a human longing to belong, a yearning to be acknowledged as "family." Part of what is fulfilled by belonging to a congregational community is a sense of affiliation. It's an interesting word, *affiliation*. Its meaning is in three letters, f-i-l, from the Latin *filius*, which means "son," and *filia*, signifying "daughter." In Roman times, affiliation was the legal procedure for adopting a child. To be church is to offer places for affiliation, where sons and daughters can find meaning for their lives.

This story in the Bible may be very familiar to you. It is usually called "The Prodigal Son." Like Jesus' other parables, this one is relatively short and entices its readers to supply details and nuances beyond the text. What is left unsaid can invite us as readers to "imagine in."

Like Jesus' other parables, this one is another puzzling answer to a general puzzle, "What is this Kingdom you keep preaching?" Jesus seems to be responding to his critics who repeatedly murmured (Lk. 15:2): "This man [this supposed messiah] welcomes sinners and eats with them."

Hear that one short sentence as an eerie, echoing counterpoint through centuries of church history since. The creeds we recite in worship date from later centuries; if there had been a creed during Jesus' lifetime, it likely could have included these words: "This man welcomes sinners and eats with them." How might the church have been different during those centuries, and in our time, with such a creed? Could we stand to recite it?

Jesus was saying in his parable that the father's kind of relentless, uncalculating redemption was the very heart of the gospel. Does such redemption happen? My favorite line in Jesus' parable is in verse 17: "He came to himself" (NRSV).

As a kid in the 1950s, I grew up watching (and reenacting) cowboy Western movies. The characters were always getting shot, even killed, without any blood lost. They got knocked unconscious, and then they regained consciousness—"came to"—when the plot needed them back.

As a slightly older kid in the 1960s, I was a soldier in Vietnam and saw real-life mayhem, including wounds caused by gunshots and shrapnel and fear. I had a few such moments of my own. I hit bottom spiritually, I "came to" myself, and started a long walk back, to images and lessons learned in Sunday school.

Arriving just after the Tet offensive, I was in Vietnam for '68 and '69. Patriotism was mostly long gone and even a sense of purpose seemed worn out. Winning was getting yourself back home, healthy and whole; heroism was helping your buddies get home relatively whole.

When I think about that war, its defeats were not coordinates on a map but all those names in the deepest middle of the Wall memorial in Washington. (The earliest casualties are etched at both ends of the Wall, and the last are listed near its midline.) Those names are victims of electoral politics, who died in the months after our supposed leaders had concluded the war was not only pointless and unwinnable but too embarrassing to abandon.

Returning to the States, some looked at us who were veterans with pity. Some assumed we were addicted or violent. Some thought we might be comforted by the delusions of many non-veterans, unchecked by any firsthand experience. Many of them believed that the American cause in the war had been a just and glorious one.

Those of us who knew better—and some had bought their knowledge dearly—just wanted to be left alone, to lose ourselves in whatever passed for 1970s normality. The nation had moved along during our time away; talking about the war just took me back there, and what I wanted was to blend back in as quietly as possible. Most of us would not even have imagined the full welcome of Luke 15—the father who came running—as a possibility.

This parable sometimes gets cited in lengthy discussions about grace and forgiveness, but it appeals to me more as a story about being a family. As we aspire to be God's church, how can people who have made very different life-choices still function as "family"—and as church—to and for one another? Is our role model still "this man [who] welcomes sinners and eats with them"?

It helps me to think of not being purely a "prodigal" or exclusively an "older sibling," but as a complex soul in whom these characters can be found, manifesting themselves in different situations. The father who runs out to embrace his younger son upon his return also leaves the party to reconcile with his older son. One son needing forgiveness; the other son needing to forgive. We are both. As such, we all need to participate in the independent sides of God's equation of grace: "Forgive us our sins as we forgive others."

The more we have sacrificed for our own choices, the more our tendency to question why others did not sacrifice as we did. This can lead us to resent those who made different choices. How can we move beyond our pasts, "come to" ourselves, and remember who we really are in relationship to the God who saves us all?

As I noted above, parables are stories without tight borders, enticing readers to elaborate. The writer of Luke gives the father the last line, but experience tells us that this wouldn't have been the last word. What is your version of a next verse—Luke 15:33, let's call it? My version is: "And the elder brother came to himself, remembered, and then he…"

Each of us is presented with this invitation, this opportunity to welcome and be welcomed, to come home and become home.

Further Reading

Having read this book, you may have further interest in some of its topics. I have included some suggestions and information about books that are connected to this area of interest and ministry.

This book is deeply indebted to the work of pastoral theologian Dr. Carrie Doehring, a leading scholar in the development of the pastoral care method known as the intercultural care approach. Her seminal work, *The Practice of Pastoral Care,* first published in 2006 and with an expanded and revised edition published in 2014, provides extensive insight into how to provide self-reflexive, compassionate care.

In chapter 3, this book explored intense stress and the potential consequences. One source of stress that is particularly important for congregations to be aware of and engaged with is what is now commonly referred to as moral injury. The foundational work on this topic, *Soul Repair: Recovering from Moral Injury after War,* written by Rita Nakashima Brock and Gabriella Lettini, was published in 2012. To find out more about the ongoing efforts on combat moral injury, check out the Soul Repair Center at Brite Divinity School http://brite.edu/academics/programs/soul-repair/.

If you are looking for a practical handbook for supporting veterans and military families, the best book out there may be *Courage after Fire,* written by Keith Armstrong and others, published in 2005. These same authors also wrote a follow-up book entitled *Courage after Fire for Parents of Service Members,* published in 2013.

Two authors who contributed to this book, Benjamin Peters and Logan Mehl-Laituri, have published their own books. Peters' 2014 book *Through All the Plain* explores his experience as a Marine in Iraq. Mehl-Laituri's 2012 book *Reborn on the Fourth of July: The Challenge of Faith, Patriotism and Conscience,* recounts his personal experience with the war in Iraq as a soldier.

Two authors with journalism backgrounds, Chris Hedges and David Finkel, both have multiple publications and have contributed a great deal to our understanding. Hedges' 2003 book *What Every Person Should Know about War* is a thorough response to frequently asked questions about military service and war. Finkel's two books, *The Good Soldiers* (2010) and *Thank You for Your Service* (2013), are vivid retellings of stories of military service and homecoming.

There are many other great books in this area of interest, but these few suggestions offer a starting point.

Resources

Hotlines

Military One Source   800.342.9647

For active and reserve duty service members and their families; therapy and consulting sessions are provided at no cost. More information available at http://www.militaryonesource.mil/

Veterans Crisis Line   800.273.8255

Confidential support for active and reserve service members, veterans, and military family members. More information available at http://www.veteranscrisisline.net/

Safe Helpline   877.995.5247

A leading organization in supporting survivors of military sexual assault. More information available at https://www.safehelpline.org

Websites

http://www.caregiver.va.gov/

Veterans Affairs (VA) offers a number of useful resources online, including this site that provides information for those caring for veterans. Like any large institution, the VA can be hard to navigate. You may have an opportunity to accompany a veteran or family member in the process of getting care or other entitlements from the VA. The more you can educate yourself on how this system works, the better you will be in a supporting role.

http://www.oefoif.va.gov/

One of the VA's initiatives for returning service members is called Seamless Transition. This website will provide some useful information about services and opportunities for service members who served in Afghanistan and Iraq.

http://www.vetcenter.va.gov/

Vet Centers are another recent initiative by the VA. These programs are smaller and hopefully more accessible than the VA hospital system, and seek to provide mental health services at the community level.

http://www.ptsd.va.gov/

The National Center for PTSD is a leading resource in research and other information about trauma and recovery.

http://careforthetroops.org/

Care For The Troops is an organization run by a former military chaplain that seeks to strengthen mental health support for returning troops and their families. The organization has a list of "Veteran Friendly Congregations" and would be happy to expand its network by including your church, if you are interested.

http://brite.edu/academics/programs/soul-repair/

Soul Repair Center is a program of Brite Divinity School, led by Dr. Rita Nakashima Brock, a leading theologian on the topic of moral injury. The organization leads conferences and consultations around the country for congregations, mental health professionals, military chaplains, and others interested in better responding to the consequences of moral injury.

★ ★ ★

Let's build a movement together!

Join us online at
ComingHomeChurch.com

The content of this book is just a beginning. It is designed to support and energize the ministry of your congregation, and you are encouraged to engage in study and conversation within community. We want to invite you to continue those conversations and explore with others around the country your ideas and best practices. Raise questions, receive feedback, and hear what other communities are doing and how to connect and partner with them. ComingHomeChurch.com is designed to bring together those committed to this important ministry for networking, partnering, and inspiration.

★ ★ ★